sensual crochet

FOR SANDRA

STERLING and the distinctive Sterling logo are registered
trademarks of Sterling Publishing Co., Inc.

Library of Congress Cataloging-in-Publication Data Available

10 9 8 7 6 5 4 3 2 1

HOLLAN Produced by Hollan Publishing, Inc.
100 Cummings Center, Suite 125G
Beverly, MA 01915
© 2008 by Hollan Publishing, Inc.

Published by Sterling Publishing Co., Inc.
387 Park Avenue South, New York, NY 10016

Distributed in Canada by Sterling Publishing
c/o Canadian Manda Group, 165 Dufferin Street
Toronto, Ontario, Canada M6K 3H6

Distributed in the United Kingdom by GMC Distribution Services
Castle Place, 166 High Street,
Lewes, East Sussex, England BN7 1XU

Distributed in Australia by Capricorn Link (Australia) Pty. Ltd.
P.O. Box 704, Windsor, NSW 2756, Australia

Printed in China

Sterling ISBN-13: 978-1-4027-4919-3
        ISBN-10: 1-4027-4919-8

For information about custom editions, special sales, premium
and corporate purchases, please contact Sterling Special Sales
Department at 800-805-5489 or specialsales@sterlingpub.com.

PHOTOGRAPHY BY ALLAN PENN

COVER AND INTERIOR DESIGN BY KARLA BAKER

CROCHET ILLUSTRATIONS BY AMY SWENSON AND
KARA GOTT

sensual crochet

LUXURIOUS YARNS, ALLURING DESIGNS

amy swenson

STERLING/HOLLAN

An imprint of Sterling Publishing Co., Inc.

New York / London
www.sterlingpublishing.com

[CONTENTS]

INTRODUCTION

Any art in which you use your hands has an implicit tactile pleasure. Working with fine yarns to create luxurious garments is, in my opinion, one of the most enjoyable ways to spend time. From angora to silk, selecting a delicious yarn for your next crochet project makes every second the yarn slips through your hands a delightful experience.

One of the goals of this book is to provide you with modern, fashionable garment designs using traditional crochet stitches. Crochet creates a freeform, lacy fabric structure that has amazing drape and drama. It's perfectly suited to sexy camisoles, seductive skirts, sensual dresses, dramatic cardigans, and dressy accessories. In *Sensual Crochet*, crochet meets catwalk.

While most of the designs in this book may seem challenging, because they use variations on the simplest of crochet stitches they are accessible for even newer crochet addicts. If you know

how to hold a hook and can whip off the basic single and double crochet stitches, you'll be set to create any of the stunning designs on the following pages.

Sensual Crochet features high-fashion garment patterns using luxury fibers: merino, cashmere, angora, alpaca, and more. These pieces are designed to feel exquisite against the skin, to allow you to showcase your crochet skills, and most important, to provide you with a garment that you'll love to wear for years to come.

Luxury does not have to mean "expensive." While it would be tough to create a cashmere garment for under $50, many of the projects in this book were chosen to make the most of just a few skeins of pricey yarns, allowing you to get your inner diva on with even a limited budget.

Whatever you decide, make sure to choose yarns you love. Life is just too short to crochet with ugly yarn.

LUXURY YARNS

Throughout this book, you'll notice that patterns feature yarns with mostly natural fiber sources. This means you're not likely to see acrylic, nylon, or other synthetics. Instead, we focus on some of the finest yarns you can find at your favorite local yarn store.

All yarns specify their fiber content. In some cases, it will be as simple as 100% cashmere. However, blended yarns that contain more than one type of fiber are increasingly popular as a way to combine the best attributes of several fiber sources. For example, a yarn blended from silk and merino will have the stretch of wool and the shine of silk.

While you'll achieve the best results by selecting the original yarn specified in the pattern, clever substitution is made easier by understanding the properties of each fiber. For example, the soft loft of pure angora will create a much different fabric than the sheen, weight, and strength of pure silk. When in doubt, work an ample swatch before beginning any project. Make sure you love the feel, weight, and drape of the fabric before continuing.

MERINO WOOL

Just the word "wool" may instantly conjure images of coarse and scratchy sweaters. However, wool can be as fine and soft as expensive cashmere, at a fraction of the cost. The breed of sheep from which the wool is shorn has a lot to do with the final quality of the yarn. Wool coming from merino sheep is generally considered the finest and softest widely available wool fiber. When shopping, look for yarns labeled "100% Pure Merino," "New Merino," or "Super-fine Merino."

CASHMERE

Cashmere, long known as the "crème de la crème" of luxury fibers, is exceptionally soft and lightweight. Don't be surprised if a 50g skein of cashmere contains far more yards than a 50g skein of the same thickness of merino. Most of the world's cashmere is plucked or shed from the soft undercoats of Mongolian and Chinese goats. Just as these undercoats keep the goats toasty during the harsh Himalayan winters, cashmere yarns will keep you warm and cozy while feeling exquisite against your most delicate skin.

ANGORA

Angora fiber is shorn from Angora rabbits. The long fur is exceptionally soft and silky. Angora fabric tends to shed constantly unless combined with a more resilient fiber such as silk, wool, or alpaca. Angora is quite warm, and makes feminine and sensual fabrics, suitable for any use.

ALPACA

Originating primarily from South America, alpaca fiber can be one of the best buys for crocheters who have expensive tastes on a tight budget. Alpaca yarn is often softer than merino wool, and is usually a fraction of the price. Even better, butter-soft alpaca yarn is exceptionally warm. The fibers are hollow at the center, trapping air and providing an insulating effect, much like a Thermos. Alpaca yarn is currently experiencing a bit of a renaissance, and can be found nearly everywhere. Don't miss the exceptional blends of alpaca with other fibers such as silk, cashmere, and merino.

MOHAIR

Mohair, which also originates from goat hair, is strong and thin by nature. Commercially available mohair ranges from bulky and relatively hairy to gossamer-weight fluff. The softest mohair comes from goats 18 months old or younger, and is typically labeled "Kid Mohair." While it's possible to find 100% mohair yarns, more commonly mohair is blended or spun with wool, silk, or other fibers to combine the shine and halo of the mohair while giving the yarn some body or thickness with the other fiber.

SILK

Silk comes from moth cocoons, and can be harvested either from already broken cocoons or before the silk worm emerges. Long prized for its shine, strength, and beautiful drape, silk is one of the most enjoyable and interesting pure fibers with which to work. Many of the patterns in this book feature pure silk yarns, but silk can also be combined quite effectively with everything from alpaca to yak.

EXOTIC ALTERNATIVES

Luxury fiber sources can be found elsewhere as well. In recent years, yarn producers have been looking to alternatives to animal-based fiber. Bamboo fiber has a sheen and drape similar to silk, yet feels deliciously lightweight against the skin—perfect for warm-weather wear. Fine linen and cotton also come from plant fibers, and are equally well suited for any crochet endeavors. Soybean plants are even being used for yarn sources; "soy silk," another silklike fiber, is glossy and slinky.

HOW TO USE THE PATTERNS

The crochet patterns in this book are geared toward advanced beginners and expert crocheters alike. For the most part, patterns use shaping, gorgeous stitch patterns, and fine-gauge yarns to obtain a luxurious finished product. However, if you are able to work the basic crochet stitches, don't hesitate to try any of the projects in this book! One of the secrets of crochet is that once you're comfortable with chain, slip stitch, single and double crochet, everything else comes pretty naturally.

The other secret is that patterns aren't easy or difficult, just short or long in the time they take to complete. Because nearly every line of a crochet pattern needs to be explicitly outlined, as long as you can read the instructions, you'll be able to follow along.

PATTERN FORMAT

Every pattern in this book follows a consistent format, which experienced crocheters should easily recognize. You'll find a quick introduction to the design, followed by the equipment, materials, gauge, and project instructions. At the project's end there will be additional instructions or information you need to properly finish your garment.

THE IMPORTANCE OF GAUGE

No one likes to make gauge swatches, but it's an essential part of beginning any crochet project. If the size of your stitches varies even slightly from the stated gauge, the finished size of your project will vary as well. For example, if a project specifies that you need 12 single crochet stitches to obtain a piece of fabric 4" wide, and you only have 10 to 4", the camisole that you'd hoped would be 32" around will be more like 39" around.

Be sure to check your gauge and re-work your swatch as necessary until you obtain the proper gauge. For patterns where gauge is provided over a specific stitch pattern, instructions will be provided to tell you exactly how your swatch should be completed.

For example:

To work gauge swatch, ch 25. Work rows 1–5 of stitch pattern once, then rows 2–5 once more. Wet block and let dry. Swatch, when measured, should be 4.5" wide and 4" tall.

If your gauge swatch is smaller than indicated after blocking, move up to a larger hook size. If it's quite large, switch to a smaller hook. The hook sizes listed in each pattern are what the designer used. However, because every crocheter has a different style, it's perfectly fine to use the hook size you need to obtain the correct gauge.

Because the same US hook letter name can be used for multiple millimeter sizes, be sure to check the size of your hooks carefully and compare them to the pattern. For example, a G hook can range from 4.0mm to 4.5mm. Patterns in this book specify the hook size in both US sizes and metric sizes.

BLOCKING

When swatching for crochet, it's incredibly important to also *block* your completed swatch before measuring. As most crochet creates a lacelike fabric, blocking the swatch will dramatically change the size and look of the fabric. All projects in this book are designed to be blocked after finishing for the most professional results.

To wet block crochet, fill a sink or bowl with room-temperature water. Submerse the fabric until fully saturated. Be especially careful at this point not to agitate the water, or your yarn may begin to shrink.

Remove the piece from the water and get rid of excess water by letting it drip or gently squeezing it. Lay flat on a towel and gently stretch into the desired shape. If an exceptionally open lace is desired, you can use rust-proof pins to stretch the fabric to the shape and size you want.

For delicate yarns that may shrink or mat when subjected to this kind of treatment, you may wish to steam or spray block instead. A pure cashmere yarn, for example, may react better to this gentle treatment.

For steam blocking, set your iron to its steam setting. Lay your piece, or pieces, on a towel and cover with a thin piece of fabric, such as a tea towel or kitchen towel. Hover the iron over the fabric layers until the crochet feels warm and damp. Do not press. Remove the fabric and use your hands to gently manipulate the piece into the desired size and shape. Pin evenly as needed, and let dry.

Spray blocking works in much the same way, but without the heat. You'll first lay out your crochet and take a water spray bottle to finely mist the surfaces.

When damp, again use your hands to manipulate into the desired size and shape. Pin evenly as needed, and let dry.

MATERIALS AND YARN

Each pattern recommends the exact yarn used to create the photographed project. However, because not all yarns are available in every yarn shop, we've also provided some information for yarn substitution. Each pattern will list the yarn requirements in generic terms.

For example:

Approximately 400 yds worsted-weight merino. Look for yarn that knits to 18–20 sts to 4".

Because few yarn manufacturers list a recommended crochet gauge on ball bands, we also give the standard gauge in knitting terms. This will help you select an appropriate yarn on your next yarn shop visit.

SCHEMATICS AND SIZING

Choosing the correct size is the first major decision you need to make when starting a new project. Most of the garments are provided in finished sizes roughly corresponding to women's sizes 2–16. But, please don't rely on our Small, Medium, Large sizing system. Instead, use the finished measurements to help you select the proper size.

Each of the garments feature a schematic that lists the important measurements in every size included in the design. For example, with a simple cardigan, you'll find measurements for the chest circumference, the armhole depth, and the sleeve length to the underarm, as well as the body length to the underarm.

NORTH AMERICAN AND UK TERMINOLOGY

North American	UK
Slip Stitch	Slip Stitch
Single Crochet	Double Crochet
Double Crochet	Treble Crochet
Treble/Triple Crochet	Double-Treble Crochet

FOR MORE INFORMATION

Need a refresher in your crochet abbreviations? Curious about more resources? The last section of this book features a host of handy references.

To determine which size will fit you the best, first think about fit. Should the piece be worn quite close to the body, or will you be layering over a top or dress? The difference between the finished measurements and your actual body measurements is called *ease*. So, to select the correct size, first measure your actual chest measurements, then select the size closest to the amount of ease you'd like to have.

Because this book features mainly close-fitting garments, for the best results, select the size closest to your actual body measurements or a bit smaller, especially for cardigans designed to be worn open. If the pattern has any specific fit or sizing tips, notes will be included in the pattern text. For example, if a cardigan or wrap is meant to be oversized, a note in the pattern introduction will indicate this. You will have vastly different results if you choose a size that fits you snugly.

For scarves, wraps, and simply shaped garments, you may not see a sizing schematic. In this case, use the information provided under "Finished Measurements" to help you select the most appropriate size.

DIAGRAMS AND SYMBOLCRAFT

Where appropriate, the patterns will contain Symbolcraft charts for any complex stitch patterns. These are designed to be used in conjunction with the row-by-row written instructions. All Symbolcraft symbol definitions can be found in the Abbreviations section of the book, page 140.

This book uses standard North American terminology and symbols throughout. These differ from what's commonly used in the UK, Europe, Australia, and other parts of the world. For a quick translation, see the sidebar.

CHAPTER ONE

EVERYDAY LUXURY

*projects designed to bring elegance
to your life, every day of the week*

silken shells
COWL

amy swenson

I love this sort of design. This sweater has a supersimple shape that shows off a lovely stitch and a gorgeous yarn, and it fits beautifully. It's crocheted in a Shell Trellis Lace pattern using Artyarns Silk Rhapsody, a stranded yarn—one in which the individual components are not twisted, but simply held together. The effect is much like what you'd get by holding one strand of mohair and a thicker strand of pure silk. Because it comes from a yarn dyeing company, the colors on each strand are perfectly and subtly paired.

pattern notes

This stitch pattern is exceptionally stretchy. So you might want to select a size close to (or smaller than) your actual bust measurements for a slinky, sexy fit.

For this design, it's especially important to fully pin block your swatch before settling on a hook size. The difference between an unblocked and blocked swatch can be up to 2" in this stitch pattern!

SIZES

XS (S, M, L, XL)

FINISHED MEASUREMENTS

CHEST: 30 (34, 38, 42, 46)"

TOTAL LENGTH: 33 (33, 33, 35, 35)"

LENGTH NOT INCLUDING COWL:
24½ (24½, 24½, 26½, 26½)"

YARN

Artyarns Silk Rhapsody (100% silk and 30% silk, 70% kid mohair; 260yds/100g): 3 (3, 3, 4, 4) skeins, color RH130

SUBSTITUTION: Approximately 612 (689, 766, 848, 930) yds each of a lace-weight mohair and a pure silk DK-weight yarn that knits to 22–24 sts/4".

HOOKS

US G/4.0mm crochet hook, or size needed to obtain proper gauge

NOTIONS

Yarn needle

GAUGE

To work a proper gauge swatch for this project:

Ch 25 sts. Work rows 1–5 of st pattern, then repeat rows 2–5 once. Fasten off.

Wet block, stretching slightly so lace pattern is open and flat.

Your swatch should measure 4½" wide and 4½" tall.

SILKEN SHELLS COWL

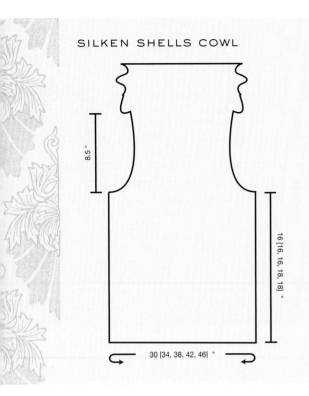

FRONT AND BACK

Make 2.

Ch 85 (97, 109, 121, 133).

Work Shell Trellis Lace Pattern rows 1–5, then work rows 2–5 7 (7, 7, 8, 8) times, ending having just finished row 5 of pattern.

ARMHOLE SHAPING

ROW 1: Work as for row 2 to last 5-dc shell cluster. Sc in center dc of cluster. Turn.

ROW 2: Work as for row 3 to last 3 ch-5-sp, sc in ch-5-sp, ch 2, dc in next sc. Turn.

Continue to work even in pattern as established to 17" from beginning of armhole shaping, ending with row 3 or 5.

FINAL ROW: Ch 1, sc in 1st st, continue as for row 2, EXCEPT, work ch 3 instead of ch 5 for a smooth edge.

FINISHING

Wet block completely and let dry before seaming for proper fit.

Sew side seams from hem to underarm. Measure up 8.5" from beginning of underarm or to desired shoulder placement. Sew sides of cowl from this point to the top of the piece. Block again, if desired.

SHELL TRELLIS LACE PATTERN

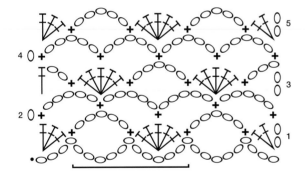

rose wrap
SHELL

robyn chachula

SIZES

XS (S, M, L, XL)

FINISHED MEASUREMENTS

CHEST: 30 (35, 38, 42, 45)"

YARN

Artyarns Regal Silk (100% hand-painted silk; 163yds/50g): 5 (6, 6, 7, 7) hanks, Soft Black (#246)

SUBSTITUTION: Approximately 700 (800, 850, 950, 1000) yds DK-weight silk that knits to 20 sts/4" in stockinette stitch on US 7 needles.

HOOKS

FOR S AND L: US G/4.25mm crochet hook

FOR XS, M, AND XL: US H/5.0mm crochet hook

NOTIONS

Yarn and sewing needles

4 ¼"-diameter pearl buttons

2 small hook and eye closures

6" of ¼" grosgrain black ribbon and matching thread

GAUGE

One granny square measures 3⅛" square on G hook and 3⅜" square on H hook.

When I think of feminine details, I think lace. Lace is flowery and light and looks complicated to create. But as I will show you in this pattern, if you can master a granny square, you can master even the most complex-looking modular lace. The Rose Wrap shell uses small circular motifs that are joined by crocheting the pieces together.

This wrap top is made sultry by the pure silk yarn. So not only do you get flowery lace, but you also get a sexy drape for a very feminine look, suitable for dramatic daywear or a night on the town.

pattern notes

A well-fitted top depends on gauge for this pattern. Use the hook size needed to achieve the correct gauge for your size.

Robyn's day job is designing structural renovations and restorations of existing buildings, which may seem like a far cry from crochet fashion design. But for her, they are one and the same. They both use her ability to take a big project and break it down into little items that she can understand, then piece them back together for the overall big picture. You can see more of her architecturally inspired pieces and Cincinnati-inspired ideas at www.crochetbyfaye.com.

SPECIAL STITCHES

DC2TOG: yo, insert hook into circle, yo, draw up loop, yo, draw through 2 loops on hook, yo, insert hook into circle, yo, draw up loop, yo, draw through 2 loops on hook, yo, draw through remaining 3 loops on hook

CL (CLUSTER): yo, (insert hook into circle, yo, draw up loop, yo, draw through 2 loops on hook) 3 times total, yo, draw through remaining 4 loops on hook

PICOT: ch 3, sl st to first ch

GRANNY SQUARE

Make 24 (40, 40, 72, 72). See Stitch Diagram for assistance.

Ch 6, join with sl st to form a ring.

ROUND 1 (RS): Ch 2, dc2tog in ring, (ch 3, cl) in ring 7 times total, ch 1, hdc into top of dc2tog.

ROUND 2: (Ch 5, sc into top of ch-sp) 7 times total, ch 2, dc into hdc on previous round.

ROUND 3: *Ch 5, (cl, ch 3, cl) into next ch-5-sp, ch 5, sc in next ch-5-sp*, repeat from * to * for a total of 3 times, ch 5, (cl, ch 3, cl) into next ch-5-sp, ch 2, dc into dc of previous round.

ROUND 4: *Ch 5, sc into next ch-5-sp, ch 5, sc into ch-3-sp, ch 5, sc into ch-3-sp, ch 5, sc into next ch-5-sp*, repeat from * to * for a total of 4 times. Fasten off. Weave in ends.

TRIANGLE GRANNY SQUARE

Make 4 (6, 6, 6, 6). See Stitch Diagram for assistance.

Ch 6, join with sl st to form a ring.

ROUND 1 (RS): Ch 2, dc in ring, (ch 3, cl) in ring 3 times total, ch 3, dc2tog in ring, turn.

ROUND 2: (Ch 5, sc into top of ch-3-sp) 4 times total, ch 3, hdc into dc on previous round, turn.

ROUND 3: Ch 6, cl in ch-3-sp, ch 5, sc in next ch-5-sp, ch 5, (cl, ch 3, cl) into next ch-5-sp, ch 5, sc in next ch-5, ch 5, (cl, ch 2, tr) into next ch-5-sp, turn.

ROUND 4: Ch 4, sc into ch-2-sp, (ch 5, sc into next ch-5-sp) twice, ch 5, sc into ch-3-sp, ch 5, sc into ch-3-sp, (ch 5, sc into next ch-5-sp) 3 times, ch 4, sl st in same ch-5-sp. Fasten off. Weave in ends.

HALF GRANNY SQUARE

Make 15 (16, 16, 4, 4). See Stitch Diagram for assistance.

Ch 6, join with sl st to form a ring.

ROUND 1 (RS): Ch 2, dc in ring, (ch 3, cl) in ring 3 times total, ch 3, dc2tog in ring, turn.

ROUND 2: (Ch 5, sc into top of ch-3-sp) 4 times total, ch 3, hdc into dc on previous round, turn.

GRANNY SQUARE

TRIANGLE GRANNY SQUARE

HALF GRANNY SQUARE

THREE-QUARTER GRANNY SQUARE

ROUND 3: Ch 1, sc in ch-3-sp, [ch 5, (cl, ch 3, cl) into next ch-5-sp, ch 5, sc in next ch-5-sp] twice, turn.

ROUND 4: Ch 5, sc into ch-5-sp, ch 5, sc into ch-3-sp, ch 5, sc into ch-3-sp, (ch 5, sc into next ch-5-sp) 2 times, ch 5, sc into ch-3-sp, ch 5, sc into ch-3-sp, ch 5, sc into next ch-5-sp, ch 5, sl st in sc. Fasten off. Weave in ends.

THREE-QUARTER GRANNY SQUARE

Make 2 (0, 0, 2, 2). See Stitch Diagram for assistance.

Ch 6, join with sl st to form a ring.

ROUND 1 (RS): Ch 2, dc in ring, (ch 3, cl) in ring 4 times total, ch 3, dc2tog in ring, turn.

ROUND 2: (Ch 5, sc into top of ch-3-sp) 5 times total, ch 3, hdc into dc on previous round, turn.

ROUND 3: Ch 1, sc in ch-3-sp, [ch 5, (cl, ch 3, cl) into next ch-5-sp, ch 5, sc in next ch-5-sp] twice, ch 5, (cl, ch 2, tr) in last ch-5-sp, turn.

ROUND 4: Ch 5, sc in ch-2-sp, *[ch 5, sc into ch-5-sp] twice, ch 5, sc into ch-3-sp, ch 5, sc into ch-3-sp,* repeat from * to * once more, ch 5, sc into ch-5-sp, ch 5, sl st in sc. Fasten off. Weave in ends.

ASSEMBLY

Arrange all motifs per corresponding size layouts. Join motifs as follows.

JOINING 4 GRANNY SQUARES

Ch 6, join with sl st to form a ring, ch 2, dc2tog in ring, *ch 1, sc in ch-5-sp of corner of granny, ch 1, cl in ring, ch 3, cl in ring*, 3 times total, ch 1, sc in ch-5-sp of corner of granny, ch 1, cl in ring, ch 1, hdc into top of dc2tog, (center made) dc into next ch-5-sp of first granny, ch 3, sc into next ch-5-sp of next granny, ch 3, sc into previous ch-5-sp of first granny, *ch 3, sc into next ch-5-sp of next granny, ch 3, sc into next ch-5-sp of first granny*, repeat from * to * 2 times total, ch 5, sc into last ch-5-sp of next granny. Fasten off. Weave in ends.

JOINING BETWEEN CENTERS

Join yarn to a ch-3-sp of first center, dc into next ch-5-sp of first granny, ch 3, sc into next ch-5-sp of next granny, ch 3, sc into previous ch-5-sp of first granny, *ch 3, sc into next ch-5-sp of next granny, ch 3, sc into next ch-5-sp of first granny*, repeat from * to * 2 times total, ch 3, sc into ch-3-sp of next center, ch 3, sc into last ch-5-sp of next granny. Fasten off. Weave in ends.

JOINING AT ARM, NECK, OR BOTTOM EDGE OF 2 GRANNY SQUARES

Join yarn to a ch-3-sp of first center, dc into next ch-5-sp of first granny, ch 3, sc into next ch-5-sp of next granny, ch 3, sc into previous ch-5-sp of first granny, *ch 3, sc into next ch-5-sp of next granny, ch 3, sc into next ch-5-sp of first granny*, repeat from * to * 2 times total, ch 3, sc into ch-5-sp of the corner of the granny, ch 3, sc into ch-5-sp of the corner of the next granny, ch 3, sl st to next ch-5-sp. Fasten off. Weave in ends.

JOINING AT NECK OR BOTTOM EDGE OF 2 HALF GRANNY SQUARES

Join yarn to a ch-3-sp of first center, dc into next ch-5-sp of first granny, ch 3, sc into next ch-5-sp of next granny, ch 3, sc into previous ch-5-sp of first granny, ch 2, sc into next ch-5-sp of the first granny, ch 3, sc into ch-5-sp of the next granny, ch 2, sl st to next ch-5-sp. Fasten off. Weave in ends.

JOINING 2 TRIANGLE GRANNY SQUARES AT NECK EDGE

Ch 6, join with sl st to form a ring, ch 3, sc in ch-5-sp of first granny, *ch 1, cl in ring, ch 1, sc in ch-5-sp of joining, ch 1, cl in ring, ch 1, sc in ch-5-sp of next granny*, twice, ch 3, sl st to circle, (half center made). Fasten off. Weave in ends.

JOINING BETWEEN CENTERS

JOINING AT EDGE

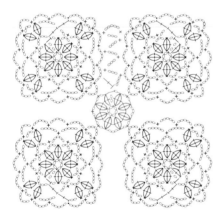

JOINING FOUR GRANNIES

JOINING AT EDGE OF HALF GRANNIES

JOINING AT HALF CENTERS

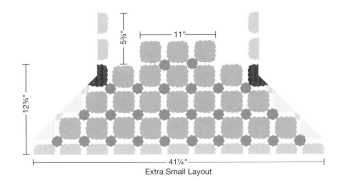

Extra Small Layout

11"
5¾"
12¾"
41¼"

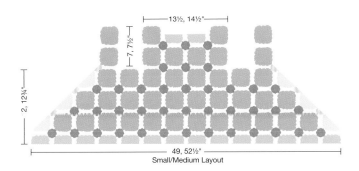

Small/Medium Layout

13½, 14½"
7, 7½"
2, 12¾"
49, 52½"

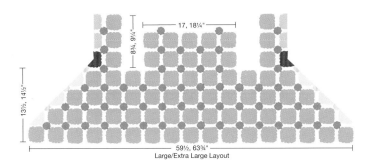

Large/Extra Large Layout

17, 18¼"
8¾, 9¼"
13½, 14½"
59½, 63¾"

FINISHING

Fold body over to line up arms. Join front arms to back at shoulder seam using joining method described above.

EDGING

With right side facing, join yarn to center bottom edge of back, (3 sc, picot) evenly around edge. Repeat for arm openings.

Cut ribbon into two pieces, one 1½" and one 4½" long.

Pin and sew ribbon to inside face of body at side seams matching front flaps.

Sew 4 buttons evenly along 4½" ribbon, making sure to line up picots of opposite edge of the outside front flap. Spaces under picots (between single crochets) become buttonholes.

Sew hook and eyes to top of inside flap and short ribbon.

ribbed surplice
TOP

annie modesitt

SIZES

XS (S, M, L, XL, 2X)

28 (32, 36, 40, 44, 50)"

FINISHED MEASUREMENTS

CHEST: 30 (34, 38, 42, 46, 52)"

YARN

YARN A: Artyarns Silk Ribbon (100% silk; 128yds/25g): 3 (3, 4, 4, 5, 5) skeins, color 133

YARN B: Artyarns Silk Rhapsody (100% silk and 30% silk, 70% mohair; 260yds/100g): 4 (4, 4, 5, 5, 5) skeins, color 133

YARN C: Artyarns Beaded Silk (100% silk with glass silver beads; 100yds/50g): 2 (2, 2, 2, 3, 3) skeins, color 133

HOOKS

US F/3.75mm hook, or size needed to obtain proper gauge

US G/4.0mm hook, or size needed to obtain proper gauge

NOTIONS

Yarn needle

GAUGE

In Waist Stitch pattern, 16 sts and 16 rows to 4" on smaller hook

In Surplice Shell pattern, 22 sts and 8 rows to 4" on smaller hook

Accented with a sparkly beaded silk yarn, this top features a crossover mohair bodice and coy elbow-length sleeves. The waistline is worked in a pure silk ribbon. This top is inspired in part by the feminine and demure, yet entirely sensual, styles of the early 1940s. Can you imagine donning this top with a pencil-slim skirt and ankle-strap high heels? The silk and beads lend an air of instant glamour, suitable for any silver-screen starlet.

pattern notes

It may be helpful to use a contrasting marker for beg of rnd (center back) to distinguish it from other markers.

If markers interfere with increases/decreases, remove them when working sts and then replace them.

Annie Modesitt enjoys the sculptural nature of crochet and the fact that beautiful fabric can be made using just a hook and a string—like catching a fish! Annie's designs and essays about knitting and crochet can be found in several books and magazines, including Interweave Crochet, Family Circle, *and* Easy Knitting. *Annie is the editor of the 2006 and 2007 Accord* Crochet Pattern-a-Day *calendars.*

RIBBED WAIST

With Yarn A and G/4.0mm hook, ch 30 (34, 38, 42, 46, 52) sts.

ROW 1: Change to F/3.75 hook.

Insert hook into 2nd ch from hook, hdc each ch. Turn.

ROW 2 (WS): Ch 1. Sc into back loop of each hdc. Turn.

ROW 3 (RS): Ch 2. Hdc into each sc.

Repeat rows 2–3 until piece measures 26 (30, 34, 38, 42, 48)"—104 (120, 136, 152, 168, 192) rows—or fits around waist and lower ribcage comfortably. End with a right side row. Fasten off.

BOTTOM EDGE

ROW 1: With Yarn C, join yarn to last st of ribbing, on right side, work along side edge of piece, working 3 sc for every 2 rows, turn.

ROW 2: Ch 1, sc into each edge sc to create a firm bottom edge of piece. Fasten off.

Fold piece in half, right sides together. Sc last row of ribbing to foundation ch, forming a tube.

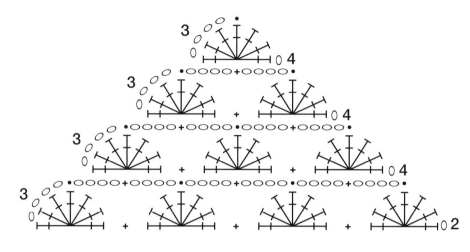

BODICE

SET UP FOR SURPLICE PATTERN

Using the seam as either a left or right side seam, mark Center Front and Center Back, mark Left Side and Right Side, mark point between Center Front and Left Side with a blue marker, mark point between Center Front and Right Sides with a red marker (these last 2 will be the beginning and end of the next surplice row).

Starting at blue marker and working with right side facing, Yarn B and size G/4.0mm hook, hdc 160 (184, 200, 224, 248, 280) sts around top of tube (side edges) back to blue marker. Continue in same direction, work in blo of row below, ending at red marker (behind original sts)—188 (220, 236, 268, 292, 332) sts, turn work.

START SHELL PATTERN

ROW 1 (WS): Ch 1, sc in each hdc to end of row (blue marker), turn.

ROW 2 (RS): *(Ch 1, skip 3, 7 dc into next st, skip 3, sc into next st), repeat from * to last 4 sts, 7 dc into next st, sc into last st, turn—24 (28, 30, 34, 37, 42) shells.

ROW 3 (WS): *(Ch 4, sl st into top of next shell, ch 4, sc into sp to left of next sc), repeat from * across, end sl st into top of last shell, turn.

ROW 4 (RS): (7 dc into next sc, sc into next sl st at top of prev row shell), repeat to end, end sl st into top of last shell, turn.

Repeat rows 3 and 4, working back and forth in shell pattern as established, creating a diagonal slant at each edge by working 1 motif in from the edge every other row as charted.

When a total of 13 (17, 19, 21, 23, 27) motifs remain, place a red marker in each edge shell [shells #1 and #13 (17, 19, 21, 23, 27)] and divide for Fronts and Back as follows:

LEFT FRONT

ROW 1 (WS): (Ch 4, sl st into top of next shell, ch 4, sc into sp to left of next sc) 1 (2, 3, 3, 3, 4) times, mark last sc worked, ch 6, sc into 2nd ch from hook, turn.

ROW 2 (RS): 7 dc into sc, sc into marked st, (7 dc into next sc, sc into next sl st at top of prev row shell), repeat to end, end sc into sl st at top of edge shell, turn.

ROW 3 (WS): (Ch 4, sl st into top of next shell, ch 4, sc into sp to left of next sc) end sl st into top of last shell, turn.

ROW 4 (RS): (7 dc into next sc, sc into next sl st at top of prev row shell), repeat to end, end sl st into top of last shell at neck edge, turn.

ROW 5 (WS): (Ch 4, sl st into top of next shell, ch 4, sc into sp to left of next sc), repeat to end, end sc into 7th dc at edge of last shell. Ch 6, sc into 2nd ch from hook, turn.

Repeat rows 2–5, dec one 7-st motif at each neck edge every 4th row as established, while adding one 7-st motif at armhole edge as indicated until only 2 (3, 4, 4, 4, 5) motifs remain.

Work even, working 2 (3, 4, 4, 4, 5) motifs in each right side row until a total of 20 (24, 28, 28, 32, 36) rows of motifs have been worked—10 (12, 14, 14, 16, 18) points along armhole edge. The last row should have a shell motif protruding at the neck.

RIGHT FRONT

With new ball of Yarn B and G hook, with wrong side facing and starting to left of 2nd (3rd, 4th, 4th, 4th, 5th) motif from neck edge, work as follows:

ROW 1 (WS): Sc into sp to left of 2nd (3rd, 4th, 4th, 4th, 5th) motif from neck edge, (ch 4, sl st into top of next shell, ch 4, sc into sp to left of next sc), repeat to end, end sl st into top of last shell at neck edge.

ROW 2 (RS): (7 dc into next sc, sc into next sl st at top of prev row shell), repeat to top of last shell (armhole edge shell) mark last sc worked. Ch 6, work 7 dc into second ch from hook, turn.

ROW 3 (WS): Ch 4, sl st into top of newly formed shell, ch 4, insert hook into top of last dc from shell and marked st, draw loop through both sts. (Ch 4, sl st into top of next shell, ch 4, sc into sp to left of next sc) end sl st into top of last shell at neck edge, turn.

ROW 4 (RS): (7 dc into next sc, sc into next sl st at top of prev row shell), repeat to armhole edge, end 7 dc into edge sc (armhole edge shell), turn.

ROW 5 (WS): (Ch 4, sl st into top of next shell, ch 4, sc into sp to left of next sc) end sl st into top of last shell at neck edge, turn.

Repeat rows 2–5, dec one 7-st motif at each neck edge every 4th row as established, while adding one 8-st motif at armhole edge as indicated until only 2 (3, 4, 4, 4, 5) motifs remain.

Work even, working 2 (3, 4, 4, 4, 5) motifs in each right side row until a total of 20 (24, 28, 28, 32, 36) rows of motifs have been worked—10 (12, 14, 14, 16, 18) points along armhole edge. The last row should have a shell motif protruding at the neck.

BACK

Return to point of armhole divide.

ROW 1 (WS): Join yarn at top of 3rd (4th, 5th, 5th, 5th, 6th) shell from front edge with a sl st, (ch 4, sc into sp to left of next sc, ch 4, sl st into top of next shell)—8 (10, 10, 12, 14, 16) motifs, ending at top of 3rd (4th, 5th, 5th, 5th, 6th) shell from edge, turn.

ROW 2 (RS): Ch 1, sc into sl st just worked, (7 dc into next sc, sc into next sl st at top of prev row shell), repeat to top of last shell, turn.

ROW 3 (WS): (Ch 4, sc into sp to left of next sc, ch 4, sl st into top of next shell), repeat to last shell in row, ending by working sc at end of last shell, turn.

ROW 4 (RS): Ch 2, dc into sc just worked, (sc into next sl st at top of prev row shell, 7 dc into next sc), repeat to end, end 7 dc into last sc of row, turn.

ROW 5 (WS): (Ch 4, sl st into top of next shell, ch 4, sc into sp to left of next sc), repeat to last shell in row, ending with sl st at top of last shell, turn.

ROW 6 (RS): (7 dc into next sc, sc into next sl st at top of prev row shell), repeat to end, end sc into next sl st at top of last shell of prev row. Work even, working 8 (10, 10, 12, 14, 16) motifs in each right side row until a total of 12 (12, 16, 16, 16, 20) rows of motifs have been worked, turn—6 (6, 8, 8, 8, 10) points along armhole edge. The last row should have a shell motif protruding at each edge.

JOIN FRONT AND BACK

Nest the shoulder edges together so that the last motif in the back extends out at either armhole edge and the peaks from the front rest between the peaks of the back. Working from the wrong side, sc shoulders together.

NECK EDGING

ROW 1 (RS): With Yarn C, starting at bottom of left neck edge, (sl st into outermost point of next shell motif, ch 4).

Repeat to and include first red-marked shell motif; move marker to just worked slipped st.

(Sl st into next "valley" between two points, ch 4), repeat to shoulder seam.

(Sl st into outermost point of next shell motif, ch 4), repeat to shoulder seam.

(Sl st into next "valley" between two points, ch 4), repeat to and include second red-marked shell motif; move marker to just worked slipped st.

(Sl st into outermost point of next shell motif, ch 4), repeat to bottom of right neck edge, turn.

ROW 2 (WS): Work 4 sc into each ch-sp, turn.

ROW 3 (RS): Sl st in 1st st, 1 sc each sc to last sc, sl st in last st.

ROW 4 (WS): Skip slipped st, sl st in next st, (1 sc into next sc), repeat to marked st.

(1 sc into each next 2 sc, sc 2tog), repeat to shoulder seam.

(1 sc into next sc), repeat to shoulder seam.

(1 sc into each next 2 sc, sc 2tog), repeat to next marked st.

(1 sc into next sc), repeat to 1 st before last sc, sl st in last st, turn.

ROW 5 (RS): Sl st in 1st st, sc 10, hdc to marked st, dc to next marked st, hdc to last 11 sc, sc 10, sl st in last st, turn.

ROW 6 (WS): Sl st in next st, (1 sc into next sc), repeat to marked st, turn.

(1 sc next st, sc 2tog), repeat to next marked st.

(1 sc into next sc), repeat to 1 st before bottom left edge, sl st in last st, turn.

ROW 7 (RS): Sl st in 1st st, sc 10, hdc to marked st, dc to next marked st, hdc to last 11 sc, sc 10, sl st in last st.

NEXT ROW (WS): Sl st in 1st st, sc to last sc, sl st in last sc.

PICOT EDGE

Worked on wrong side.

1 sc each next 3 sts, ch 3, insert hook from wrong side to right side into second sc worked and from right side back to wrong side through next unworked st, draw loop through, yo, draw loop through both loops on hook, move on to next unworked st. Fasten off.

SLEEVE

Make 2.

SLEEVE CAP

Count the "peaks" and "valleys" around each arm-hole; there should be 16 (18, 22, 22, 24, 28) points

of each. Lay piece flat, shoulder seam will be behind and below shoulder top.

Mark center bottom peak of work and, with wrong side facing, join yarn to peak immediately to the left of the center bottom peak.

ROW 1 (WS): (Ch 4, sc into valley to left of last sc, ch 4, sl st into top of next peak), repeat to last peak to the right marked peak, turn.

ROW 2 (RS): (7 dc into sc in valley, sl st at top of prev row shell) 13 (15, 19, 19, 21) times, end with 7 dc in valley before peak where yarn was joined, turn.

ROW 3 (WS): (Ch 4, sl st into top of next shell, ch 4, sc into sp to left of next sc) end sl st into top of 13th (15th, 19th, 19th, 21st) shell, turn.

ROW 4 (RS): (7 dc into sc in valley, sl st at top of prev row shell) 12 (14, 18, 18, 20) times, end dc 7 in valley before peak where yarn was joined, turn.

ROW 5 (WS): (Ch 4, sl st into top of next shell, ch 4, sc into sp to left of next sc) end sl st into top of 12th (14th, 18th, 18th, 20th) shell, turn.

Continue in this manner, working 2 fewer motifs (decreasing) in each right side row until there are a total of 9 (11, 15, 15, 17) shells. End with sl st into top of prev shell. Fasten off.

UPPER ARM

Worked in the round.

ROUND 1 (WS): Join Yarn B at bottom marked peak, and working on the wrong side, ch 4, sc into valley to left of marked peak, (ch 4, sl st into sc at top of next shell, ch 4, sc into sc at top of next shell) twice, ch 4, sl st at top of next shell, ch 4, sc into sp to left of next sc) 9 (11, 15, 15, 17) times, (ch 4, sc into sc at top of next shell, ch 4, sl st into sc at top of next shell) twice, ch 4, sc into valley to left of marked peak, ch 4, sl st into marked peak, turn.

ROUND 2 (RS): (7 dc into sc, sc into next sl st), repeat around, ending sl st into marked peak—16 (18, 22, 22, 24, 28) shells, turn.

ROUND 3 (WS): (Ch 4, sl st into top of next shell, ch 4, sc into sp to left of next sc), repeat around, end sc into sl st above marked point, turn.

ROUND 4 (RS): Ch 2, dc 3, (sc into next sl st, 7 dc into sc), repeat around, ending with 4 dc to complete shell at point where initial 3 dc was formed, turn.

ROUND 5 (WS): (Ch 4, sc into sp to left of next sc, ch 4, sl st into top of next shell), repeat around, turn.

SLEEVE DECREASES

Repeat rounds 2–5, working 6 dc shells instead of 7. Continue to repeat rounds 2–5, working 1 fewer dc in each shell in round until there are 5 dc in each shell. Work even, with no further decreasing in shells, working 5 dc in each shell until sleeve measures 10" from shoulder to sleeve edge, or desired length. End with a right side round. Fasten off.

SLEEVE EDGING

With Yarn C, work 2 rows of sc around edge of each sleeve. Fasten off.

FINISHING

Weave in all ends.

RIBBED SURPLICE SCHEMATIC

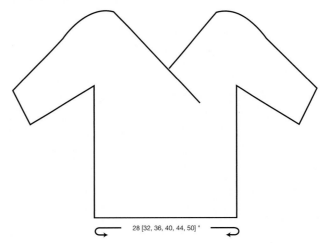

28 [32, 36, 40, 44, 50] "

butterfly
CARDIGAN

amy swenson

Deliciously delicate and absolutely addictive, this Chain Lace stitch pattern creates a lovely, modern lace. Here, a double strand of the softest and most precious alpaca yarn is used to create a stunning yet cozy open cardigan. Designed to be worn open, thrown over a lace-edge camisole for summer or a close fitting turtleneck for winter, this cardigan is versatile and stylish year round. Wide, kimono-inspired sleeves drape elegantly against a bare wrist, while the slightly cropped length perfectly sets off longer layers.

pattern notes

Exact size is controlled by firmly wet blocking and pinning into the desired measurements. Because this cardigan is meant to be worn swinging and loose, for best fit, select a finished chest measurement at least 5" larger than your actual chest size. Yarn is held double throughout pattern. Pattern is worked in one piece from back hem to front hem.

SIZES

XS–S (M–L, XL–2X)

FINISHED MEASUREMENTS

CHEST: 40 (50, 62)"

YARN

Blue Sky Alpacas Royal (100% baby alpaca; 288yds/100g): 5 (7, 9) skeins, Spanish Leather

SUBSTITUTION: Approximately 1440 (1914, 2078) yds sport-weight yarn. Look for yarn that knits to 24–26 sts/4".

HOOKS

US J/6.0mm crochet hook, or size needed to obtain proper gauge

NOTIONS

Yarn needle

Removeable stitch marker

GAUGE

To work gauge swatch:

Holding two strands of yarn together, ch 21.

Work Butterfly Chain Lace pattern rows 1–5, then rows 2–4. Cut yarn, fasten off.

Wet block and stretch, pinning into shape. Swatch should measure 6½" wide and 6" high at tallest point.

STITCH PATTERN
BUTTERFLY CHAIN LACE

Worked over a multiple of 10 sts plus 1.

ROW 1: After completing foundation chain, ch 2, dc in 3rd ch from hook, *skip 4 ch, ch 4, (sc, ch 7) 3 times in next ch, sc in same ch, skip 4 ch, ch 4, dc in next ch*. Repeat from * to *, ending with dc in final ch. Turn.

ROW 2: Ch 1, *sc in dc, ch 1, (sc in ch-7-sp, ch 3) twice, sc in ch-7-sp, ch 1*. Repeat from * to * across, ending with sc in dc. Skip turning ch. Turn.

ROW 3: Ch 1. In first sc, (ch 7, sc) twice, *skip (ch-1-sp, sc, ch-3-sp) from row below, ch 4, dc in next sc, skip (ch-3-sp, sc, ch-1-sp) from row below, ch 4, (sc, ch 7) 3 times in next sc, sc in same sc*. Repeat from * to *, ending with (sc, ch 7, sc, ch 4, dtr) in last sc. Skip turning ch, turn.

ROW 4: Ch 1. Sc in ch-7-sp, ch 3, sc in next ch-7-sp, *ch 1, sc in dc, ch 1, (sc in ch-7-sp, ch 3) twice, sc in ch-7-sp*. Repeat from * to *, ending with ch 3, sc in ch-7-sp, turn.

ROW 5: Ch 2, *dc in sc, skip (ch 3, sc, ch) from row below, ch 4, in following sc, (sc, ch 7) three times, sc in same sc, skip (ch 1, sc, ch 3) from row below, ch 4*. Repeat from * to *, ending with dc in last sc. Skip turning ch, turn.

Repeat rows 2–5 for pattern.

BACK

Ch 61 (81, 101).

Beginning with row 1 of Butterfly Chain Lace pattern, work rows 1–5, then 2–5 twice, then 2–4 once more. Do not turn at end of row.

If you'd like a longer garment, here's where to add length (before the underarm). Before blocking, piece will measure approximately 8.5" at this point.

After blocking, the distance to the underarm will be more like 12". Each repeat of rows 2–5 will add 2½" in post-blocking length.

SLEEVES

Ch 50 for 1st sleeve.

Turn, work as for row 1, placing dc in 1st sc on body. When you reach the back, continue as for row 5 to last st on body, dc in last st.

With a separate doubled strand of yarn from next set of balls, attach yarn just below stitch just made with a sl st. Ch 50. Cut yarn and fasten off.

Pick up body yarn, and continue across this ch as for row 1 of pattern.

Continue working rows 2–5 twice, then 2–4 once.

SPLIT FOR NECK

Beginning as for row 5, work 6 (7, 8) pattern repeats, dc in sc on center top of next chain cluster, ch 4, (sc, ch 7, sc, ch 4, dtr) all in 2nd sc, turn.

Both sides of piece will now be worked separately.

RIGHT SLEEVE AND FRONT

ROW 1: Ch 1, sc in ch-4-sp, ch 3, sc in ch-7-sp, ch 1, finish as for row 2 of Butterfly Chain Lace, turn.

ROW 2: Work as for row 3 to end of row, placing dc in last sc, turn.

ROWS 3–4: Continue, working as for rows 4 and 5, matching pattern as set, turn.

ROW 5: Ch 1, sc in ch-4-sp, ch 3, sc in ch-7-sp, ch 1, finish as for row 2, turn.

Continue, working as for rows 3 and 4 of Butterfly Chain Lace once more.

ADD FRONT PANEL

With a separate doubled strand of yarn, sl st to neck edge of row just worked. Ch 15, turn.

Beginning with a row 5, work in pattern across sleeve, right front, and the 15 ch sts.

Work rows 2–4. Fasten off. Do not turn.

Your right sleeve is now finished.

Without turning, reattach yarn to edge of body with sl st at underarm (22nd sc from edge, matching placement with where sleeve began on back of work).

Continue as for row 5, then repeat rows 2–5 three times, then 2–4 once. Cut yarn, fasten off.

LEFT SLEEVE AND FRONT

Sl st to attach yarn to 27th sc from sleeve edge on left side, making sure to leave 3 full ch-7 clusters for back neck. Sl st should be placed in sc above dc.

ROW 1: (Ch 8, sc, ch 7, sc) in first sc at base of sl st, ch 4, dc in next sc, continue as for row 5, turn.

Then, work rows 2–5 once and rows 2–4 once. Do not turn.

ADD FRONT PANEL

Ch 15. Turn.

ROW 1: Ch 2, dc in 3rd ch, continue as for row 5 across sleeve, left front, and the 15 ch sts, turn.

Work rows 2–4.

Place removeable stitch marker in 22nd sc from sleeve edge to indicate body edge and position for side seam.

Work as for row 5, ending with dc in marked stitch. Remove marker.

Work rows 2–5 three times, then 2–4 once (matching length for right front). Cut yarn, fasten off.

FINISHING

Wet block and pin to provided measurements. Let dry.

Sew side and underarm seams.

Weave in ends.

BUTTERFLY CARDIGAN SCHEMATIC

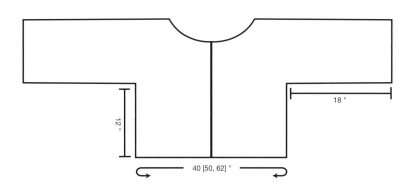

18 "

12 "

40 [50, 62] "

angel bunny
COWL

robyn chachula

SIZES
XS (S, M, L, XL)
28 (32, 36, 40, 44)"
FINISHED MEASUREMENTS
CHEST: 29¾, (34, 38¼, 42½, 46¾)"

YARN
Lorna's Laces Angel (70% angora, 30% lamb-swool; 50yds/14.25g): 21 (25, 28, 33, 35) hanks, Pewter

SUBSTITUTION: Approximately 1050 (1250, 1375, 1625, 1750) yds DK-weight angora blend that knits to 20 sts/4" in stockinette stitch.

HOOKS
US H/5.0mm crochet hook, or size needed to obtain proper gauge

NOTIONS
Yarn needle

GAUGE
4 V-st and 8 rows to 4¼" by 4" on H/5.0mm hook in stitch pattern

When I think of winter sensual, my mind immediately channels 1970s ski bunnies in fluffy sweaters. They never had to expose much skin; the sweaters' soft textures against their natural curves made it clear why they were called "bunnies." This sweater is born of that bunny essence. Whether you wear it off one or both shoulders or as a cowl, the soft halo from the angora and your own natural feminine curves will instantly turn you into a snow bunny, too.

pattern notes
Body is worked in the round to the arm openings when it is split into a front and back panel.

Stitch pattern is not blocked. This is to add some elasticity into the sweater.

Robyn's day job is designing structural renovations and restorations of existing buildings, which may seem like a far cry from crochet fashion design. But for her, they are one and the same. They both use her ability to take a big project and break it down into little items that she can understand, then piece them back together for the overall big picture. You can see more of her architecturally inspired pieces and Cincinnati-inspired ideas at www.crochetbyfaye.com.

SPECIAL STITCHES

V-ST: (2 dc, ch 3, 2 dc) in next ch-3-sp

PUFF ST: ch 4, *yo, insert hook into 4th ch from hook pull up loop* 3 times, yo, pull through 6 loops on hook, yo, pull through last two loops on hook

FDC (FOUNDATION DOUBLE CROCHET): ch 4, dc in 4th ch from hook, *dc into bottom bar of dc just made (1 chainless dc made), repeat from * for required length of fdc

ANGEL BUNNY STITCH PATTERN

Fdc 20.

SET-UP ROW: (Dc, ch 3, 2dc) in 4th ch from hook, *skip 3 ch, (2dc, ch 3, 2 dc) in next ch (V-st made)*. Repeat from * to * across, turn—5 V-sts made.

ROW 1: Ch 1, (sc, ch 3, sc) in ch-3-sp of the first V-st, *puff st, (sc, ch 3, sc) in next ch-3-sp*. Repeat from * to * across, turn—4 puff sts.

ROW 2: Ch 1, sl st in first ch-3-sp, ch 3, (dc, ch 3, 2 dc) in same ch-3-sp (counts as a V-st), *skip puff st, V-st in next ch-3-sp*. Repeat across, turn.

Repeat rows 1–2 to desired length.

BODY

Work fdc for a total of 111 (127, 143, 159, 175) dc (not incl ch-4), sl st to beginning ch to form round—112 (128, 144, 160, 176) dc total. Mark beginning of round.

EDGING

Work 3 rounds hdc.

BEGIN BUNNY STITCH PATTERN

Worked in the round without turning.

SET-UP ROUND: Ch 3, (dc, ch 3, 2dc) in first hdc, *skip 3 hdc, (2dc, ch 3, 2 dc) in next hdc (V-st made)*. Repeat around, sl st to beginning ch—28 (32, 36, 40, 44) V-sts made.

ROUND 1: Follow row 1 of stitch pattern, sl st to first sc—28 (32, 36, 40, 44) puff sts total.

ROUND 2: Repeat row 2 of stitch pattern, sl st to beginning ch—28 (32, 36, 40, 44) V-sts total.

WAIST SHAPING DECREASES

Continue to spiral without turning.

ROUND 1: Ch 1, (sc, ch 3, sc) in ch-3-sp of the first V-st, skip puff st, (sc, ch 3, sc) in ch-3-sp of the next V-st *puff st, (sc, ch 3, sc) in next ch-3-sp*. Repeat for 13 (15, 17, 19, 21) puff st, skip puff st, (sc, ch 3, sc) in ch-3-sp of the next V-st *puff st, (sc, ch 3, sc) in next ch-3-sp*. Repeat around, sl st to first sc—26 (30, 34, 38, 42) puff sts.

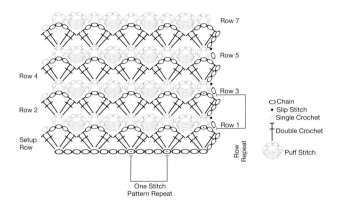

ROUND 2: Ch 1, sl st in first ch 3 sp, ch3, dc in ch 3-sp, ch 3, 2 dc in next ch-3-sp (decrease made), *skip puff st, V-st in next ch-3-sp* repeat 12 (14, 16, 18, 20) times, skip puff st, 2dc in next ch-3-sp, ch3, 2dc in next ch-3-sp, *skip puff st, V-st in next ch-3-sp* repeat around, sl to beginning ch—24 (28, 32, 36, 40) V-sts.

Repeat waist shaping rounds 1–2 once more for 12 (14, 16, 18, 20) puff sts on each side.

RETURN TO PATTERN STITCH

Repeat pattern stitch rounds 1–2 twice. Repeat round 1 once—24 (28, 32, 36, 40) puff sts.

WAIST SHAPING INCREASES

ROUND 1: Ch 1, do not turn, sl st in first ch-3-sp, ch 3, (dc, ch 3, 2 dc, ch 3, 2 dc) in same ch-3-sp (increase made), *skip puff st, V-st in next ch-3-sp* repeat for 11 (13, 15, 17, 19) V-st, skip puff st, (2 dc, ch 3, 2 dc, ch 3, 2 dc) in next ch-3-sp (increase made) *skip puff st, V-st in next ch-3-sp* repeat around, sl st to beginning ch—22 (26, 30, 34, 38) V-sts + 2 increases.

Working even, repeat rounds 1–2 of stitch pattern once. Repeat round 1 of stitch pattern once—26 (30, 34, 38, 42) puff sts.

BUST DARTS

ROUND 1: (Bust dart increase) Ch 1, do not turn, sl st in first ch-3-sp, ch 3, (dc, ch 3, 2 dc) in same ch-3-sp, *skip puff st, V-st in next ch-3-sp* repeat around for 15 (18, 21, 24, 27) V-st (not including beginning V-st), skip puff st, (2 dc, ch 3, 2 dc, ch 3, 2 dc) in next ch-3-sp (increase made) *skip puff st,

V-st in next ch-3-sp* repeat around for 6 V-st, skip puff st, (2 dc, ch 3, 2 dc, ch 3, 2 dc) in next ch-3-sp (increase made) *skip puff st, V-st in next ch-3-sp* repeat around, sl st to beginning ch—24 (28, 32, 36, 40) V-sts + 2 increases.

Repeat pattern stitch rounds 1–2 2 (3, 3, 4, 4) times—28 (32, 36, 40, 44) V-sts.

SHAPE ARMHOLE

Repeat pattern stitch round 1 once, sl to first sc (28, 32, 38, 40, 44) puff sts, *(sl st, ch1, sl st) in next ch-3, ch 4, skip puff st* repeat twice, sl st to next sc. Do not turn; you are now at the back of the work, right side facing.

BACK

We will now be working in rows and not rounds to create the back panel. The back panel is narrower than the front panel due to the bust darts.

ROW 1 (RS): Ch 1, sl st in next ch-3-sp, ch 3, (dc, ch 3, 2 dc) in same ch-3-sp, *skip puff st, V-st in next ch-3-sp* repeat across for 10 (12, 14, 16, 18) V-st (not including beginning V-st), turn—11 (13, 15, 17, 19) V-sts total.

Repeat rows 1–2 of stitch pattern 3 (4, 4, 5, 5) times. Repeat row 1 once.

BACK NECK SHAPING

RIGHT SIDE

ROW 1: Ch 1, sl st in first ch-3-sp, ch 3, (dc, ch 3, 2 dc) in same ch-3-sp (count as a V-st), *skip puff st, V-st in next ch-3-sp* repeat across for 3 V-st (not including beginning V-st), dc in next V-st, turn—4 V-sts total.

ROW 2: Ch 2, (sc, ch 3, sc) in ch-3-sp of the first V-st, *puff st, (sc, ch 3, sc) in next ch-3-sp* repeat across, turn—3 puff sts.

ROW 3: Ch 1, sl st in first ch-3-sp, ch 3, (dc, ch 3, 2 dc) in same ch-3-sp (count as a V-st), *skip puff st, V-st in next ch-3-sp* repeat across for 2 V-st (not including beginning V-st), dc in next V-st, turn—3 V-sts total.

ROW 4: Ch 2, (sc, ch 3, sc) in ch-3-sp of the first V-st, *puff st, (sc, ch 3, sc) in next ch-3-sp* repeat across, turn—2 puff sts. Fasten off, leave long tail.

LEFT SIDE

ROW 1: Skip 2 (4, 6, 8, 10) puff sts from where you fastened off. Join yarn with sl to next ch-3-sp, ch 3, *skip puff st, V-st in next ch-3-sp* repeat across, turn—4 V-sts total.

ROW 2: Repeat stitch pattern row 1—3 puff sts, turn.

ROW 3: Ch 1, (sl st, ch1, sl) in first ch-3-sp, ch 3, *skip puff st, V-st in next ch-3-sp* repeat across, turn—3 V-sts total.

ROW 4: Repeat stitch pattern row 1—2 puff sts. Fasten off. Weave in ends.

FRONT

You will be skipping a few puff sts to create another arm opening and work the front panel. Remember the front panel is wider then the back.

ROW 1: Join yarn to end of row 1 of back (right side facing) with sl st in same ch-3-sp as last V-st, ch 4, *(sl st, ch1, sl) in next ch-3, ch 4, skip puff st* repeat twice, sl st to next sc, ch 1, do not turn, ch 1, do not turn, sl st in next ch-3-sp, ch 3, (dc, ch 3, 2 dc) in same ch-3-sp, *skip puff st, V-st in next ch-3-sp* repeat across for 11 (13, 15, 17, 19) V-st (not including beginning V-st), skip puff st, (2dc, ch 3, dc) in next ch-3-sp, ch3, sl st to same ch-3-sp, dtr in next ch-3-sp (finishes arm opening), ch 3, sl st to top of previous dc, turn—13 (15, 17, 19, 21) V-sts total.

Repeat rows 1–2 of stitch pattern 3 (4, 4, 5, 5) times. Repeat row 1 once.

FRONT NECK SHAPING

RIGHT SIDE

ROW 1: Ch 1, sl st in first ch-3-sp, ch 3, (dc, ch 3, 2 dc) in same ch-3-sp (count as a V-st), *skip puff st, V-st in next ch-3-sp* repeat across for 3 V-st (not including beginning V-st), dc in next V-st, turn—4 V-sts total.

ROW 2: Ch 2, (sc, ch 3, sc) in ch-3-sp of the first V-st, *puff st, (sc, ch 3, sc) in next ch-3-sp* repeat across, turn—3 puff sts.

ROW 3: Ch 1, sl st in first ch-3-sp, ch 3, (dc, ch 3, 2 dc) in same ch-3-sp (count as a V-st), *skip puff st, V-st in next ch-3-sp*, repeat across for 2 V-st (not including beginning V-st), dc in next V-st, turn—3 V-sts total.

ROW 4: Ch 2, (sc, ch 3, sc) in ch-3-sp of the first V-st, *puff st, (sc, ch 3, sc) in next ch-3-sp*, repeat across—2 puff sts. Fasten off, leave long tail.

LEFT SIDE

ROW 1: Skip 4 (6, 8, 10, 12) puff sts, from where you fastened off, join yarn with sl st to next ch-3-sp, ch 3, *skip puff st, V-st in next ch-3-sp* repeat across, turn—4 V-sts total.

ROW 2: Repeat stitch pattern row 1—3 puff sts.

ROW 3: Ch 1, (sl st, ch1, sl st) in first ch-3-sp, ch 3, *skip puff st, V-st in next ch-3-sp* repeat across, turn—3 V-sts total.

ROW 4: Repeat stitch pattern row 1—2 puff sts. Fasten off, weave in ends.

JOIN SHOULDERS

With right sides together and using long tail at the arm side of the shoulder seam, sl st shoulders together leaving last (sc, ch 3, sc) at neck side unseamed. Sl st seam will provide extra strength for shoulder for wearability. Weave in ends.

COWL

Worked in spiraled rounds without turning.

With right back panel, right side facing, join yarn with sl st to unseamed ch-3-sp at shoulder seam.

SET-UP ROUND: Ch 3, (dc, ch 3, 2 dc) in same ch-3-sp (count as a V-st), *skip next dc, V-st in next dc, V-st in next ch-sp* repeat twice down side of neck, *skip puff st, V-st in next ch-3-sp*, repeat across back of neck, *V-st in next dc, skip dc, V-st in next ch- 3sp* twice, V-st in next ch-3-sp, *skip next dc, V-st in next dc, V-st in next ch-sp* repeat twice down side of neck, *skip puff st, V-st in next ch-3-sp*, repeat across back of neck, *V-st in next dc, skip dc, V-st in next ch 3sp* twice, sl to beginning ch—24 (28, 32, 36, 40) V-st total.

ROUND 1: Repeat row 1 of stitch pattern, sl st to first sc—24 (28, 32, 36, 40) puff sts.

ROUND 2: Repeat row 2 of stitch pattern, sl st to beginning ch—24 (28, 32, 36, 40) V-sts.

Repeat rounds 1–2 once, repeat round 1 once.

COWL INCREASES

INCREASE ROUND 1: Ch 1, sl st in first ch-3-sp, ch 3, (dc, ch 3, 2 dc, ch 3, 2 dc) in same ch-3-sp (increase made), [*skip puff st, V-st in next ch-3-sp*, repeat for 4 (5, 6, 7, 8) V-st, skip puff st, (2 dc, ch 3, 2 dc, ch 3, 2 dc) in next ch-3-sp (increase made)] repeat twice, *skip puff st, V-st in next ch-3-sp* repeat for 6 (7, 8, 9, 10) V-st, skip puff st, (2 dc, ch 3, 2 dc, ch 3, 2 dc) in next ch-3-sp (increase made), *skip puff st, V-st in next ch-3-sp* repeat around, sl st to beginning ch—20 (24, 28, 32, 36) V-sts + 4 increases.

Working even, repeat pattern st rounds 1–2 once, repeat round 1 once—28 (32, 36, 40, 44) puff sts.

INCREASE ROUND 2: Repeat Increase Round 1 above with 5 (6, 7, 8, 9) V-st between increases on back and 7 (8, 9, 10, 11) V-sts between increases on front of cowl—24 (28, 32, 36, 40) V-sts + 4 increases.

Working even, repeat pattern st rounds 1–2 three times—32 (36, 40, 44, 48) puff sts.

COWL EDGING

ROUND 1: Ch 2, do not turn, sl st in first ch-3-sp of V-st, ch 1, sc in same ch-3-sp, *ch 4, sc in next ch-3-sp* repeat around, sl st to first sc.

ROUND 2: Ch 2, *hdc in sc, 4 hdc in ch-4-sp* repeat around, sl st to first hdc.

ROUNDS 3–4: Ch 2, hdc in each hdc around.

Fasten off. Weave in ends.

SLEEVES

Work once for each sleeve. Sleeves are worked in the round without turning.

SET-UP ROUND: With right side facing, join yarn to ch-1-sp at under arm, ch 3, V-st in same sp, V-st in next ch-1-sp, 5 (6, 6, 7, 7) V-st evenly up back panel of arm, 5 (6, 6, 7, 7) V-st evenly down front panel of arm, sl st to beginning ch.

ROUND 1: Repeat row 1 of stitch pattern, sl st to first sc—12 (14, 14, 16, 16) puff sts.

ROUND 2: Repeat row 2 of stitch pattern, sl st to beginning ch—12 (14, 14, 16, 16) V-sts.

Repeat stitch pattern rounds 1–2 1 (1, 1, 2, 2) time(s).

SLEEVE DECREASES

DECREASE ROUND 1: Ch 1, (sc, ch 3, sc) in ch-3-sp of the first V-st, skip puff st, (sc, ch 3, sc) in ch-3-sp of the next V-st *puff st, (sc, ch 3, sc) in next ch-3-sp* repeat around, sl st to first sc—11 (13, 13, 15, 15) puff sts.

DECREASE ROUND 2: Ch 1, sl st in first ch-3-sp, ch 3, dc in same ch-3-sp, ch 3, 2 dc in next ch-3-sp (decrease made), *skip puff st, V-st in next ch-3-sp* repeat around, sl to beginning ch.

*Work stitch pattern rounds 1–2 twice, then Decrease Rounds 1–2 once**. Repeat from * to ** three times. Work stitch pattern rounds 1–2 once more.

SLEEVE EDGING

ROUND 1: Ch 2, sl st in first ch-3-sp of V-st, ch 1, sc in same ch-3-sp, *ch 4, sc in next ch-3-sp* repeat around, sl st to first sc.

ROUND 2: Ch 2, *hdc in sc, 4 hdc in ch-4-sp* repeat around, sl to first hdc.

ROUNDS 3–4: Ch 2, hdc in each hdc around. Fasten off. Weave in ends.

FINISHING

Weave in ends. Do not block.

ANGEL BUNNY COWL SCHEMATIC

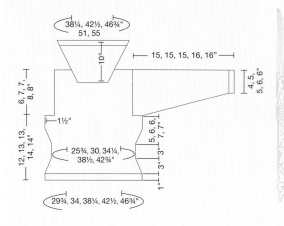

autumn berry
CARDIGAN

amy swenson

SIZES

S–M (L–XL, 2X–3X)

FINISHED MEASUREMENTS

CHEST: 37 (45, 53)"

YARN

Cascade Dolce (55% alpaca, 23% wool, 22% silk; 109yds/50g): 12 (14, 17) skeins, color 941

SUBSTITUTION: Approximately 1312 (1531, 1859) yds worsted-weight yarn. Look for yarn that knits to 20 sts/4".

HOOKS

US G7/4.5mm crochet hook, or size needed to obtain proper gauge

NOTIONS

Yarn needle

GAUGE

16 dc equals 4"

While close fitting and slinky has a definite place in my wardrobe, I also feel gorgeous in oversized, dramatic wrap sweaters. This large-scale lace pattern provides open, swingy sleeves and allows you to cozy up in style. Even better, this loose cardigan is ultrasimple. Just learn the 4-row stitch pattern and you'll fly right through it!

pattern notes

The back piece is crocheted first. Then, each front is crocheted and attached at a 90-degree angle to the back, giving a scalloped look to each front edge. Sleeves are then worked and sewn into place.

This cardigan is meant to be worn long and loose. Up to 8" of ease looks fab!

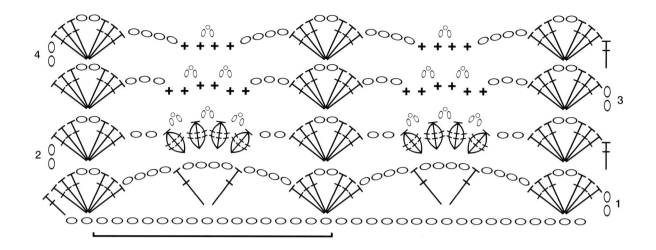

SPECIAL STITCHES

CH-2-V-ST: (3 dc, ch 2, 3 dc) in same st

CH-4-V-ST: (dc, ch 4, dc) in same st

TR-CL (TREBLE CLUSTER): yo twice and insert hook into next st, draw up loop, (yo, draw though 2 loops) twice, yo draw through 1 loop (2 loops remain) yo twice, insert hook back into same st, draw up loop, (yo draw through 2 loops) 3 times (2 loops remain), yo twice, insert hook back into same st, draw up loop, (yo draw through 2 loops) 3 times—1 cluster made

STRAWBERRY PATTERN

Worked over a multiple of 16 sts + 3.

ROW 1: After working foundation ch, ch 2. Skip 1 ch, *ch-2-V-st in next ch, ch 4, skip 7 ch, ch-4-V-st in next ch, ch 4, skip 7 ch*. Repeat from * to * across, ending with ch-2-V-st in second to last ch, dc in last ch. Turn.

ROW 2: *Ch 2, ch-2-V-st in next ch-2-sp, ch 2, skip 4 ch, (in next ch, tr-cl, ch-3) 4 times*. Repeat from * to * across, ending with ch-2-V-st in last ch-2-sp, then dc in turning ch. Turn.

ROW 3: Ch 2. *Ch-2-V-st in next ch-2-sp, ch 3, skip 2 ch, (2 sc in next ch-3-sp, ch 3) 3 times*. Repeat from * to * ending with ch-2-V-st in last ch-2-sp, then dc in turning ch once more. Turn.

ROW 4: Ch 2. *Ch-2-V-st in next ch-2-sp, ch 4, skip 3 ch, 2 sc in next ch-3-sp, ch 3, sc in next 2 sc in next ch-3-sp, ch 4*. Repeat from * to * across, ending with ch-2-V-st in last ch-2-sp, dc in turning ch. Turn.

ROW 5: Ch 2. *In next ch-2-sp, ch-2-V-st, ch 4, in next ch-3-sp, ch-4-V-st, ch 4*. Repeat from * to * across, ending with ch-2-V-st in last ch-2-sp, dc in turning ch. Turn.

Repeat rows 2–5 for pattern.

BACK

Ch 67 (83, 99).

Work rows 1–5 of Strawberry Pattern, then repeat rows 2–5 8 times, then work row 2. Fasten off.

FRONT

Make two. Fronts are worked from side edge to opening edge.

Ch 99 for all sizes.

Work rows 1–5, then rows 2–5 4 (5, 6) times, then work row 2. Fasten off.

SLEEVE

Make 2. Sleeves are worked from shoulder to cuff.

Ch 67 for all sizes.

Work rows 1–5, then rows 2–5 5 times (add a repeat for a longer sleeve), then finish with row 2. Fasten off.

FINISHING

Wet block all pieces to desired size. Back should measure 18½ (22½, 26½)" in width and 25" long after blocking. Sleeve should be 18½" in width and length as necessary. Fronts should measure 25" in width.

Back will have foundation row at bottom and final row at top of work. Fronts will have foundation chains as side seams and final row as wrap opening. Sew shoulder seams, leaving an 8½" opening in center back for neck.

Position foundation ch edge of sleeve with center at shoulder seam. Sew into place along front and back.

Sew up underarms and side seams.

Weave in ends.

AUTUMN BERRY CARDIGAN SCHEMATIC

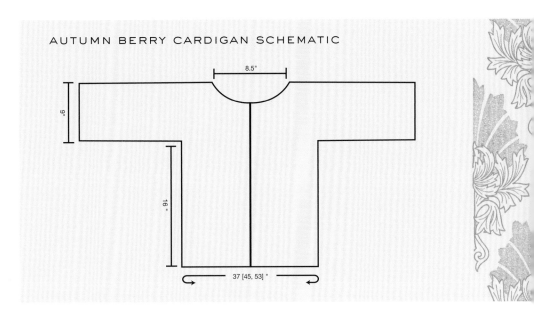

9"

16"

8.5"

37 [45, 53] "

deepest picot
CARDIGAN

amy swenson

With a super-sweet and ultimately feminine appeal, this top flatters every girlish figure. This allover lace cardigan is crocheted from Cascade Indulgence, a luscious alpaca/angora blend. It's worked from the neck down and finished with a simple tie closure. Increases along the front neck edge provide an artful point at the center front of the cardigan.

SIZES

S (M, L, XL)

FINISHED MEASUREMENTS

CHEST: 36 (40, 44, 48)"

YARN

Cascade Indulgence (70% alpaca, 30% angora; 123yds/50g): 7 (8, 9, 11) skeins, color 528

SUBSTITUTION: Approximately 875 (995, 1115, 1367) yds worsted-weight yarn. Look for yarn that knits to 20 sts/4".

HOOKS

US D/3.25mm crochet hook, or size needed to obtain proper gauge

NOTIONS

Yarn needle

GAUGE

To work gauge swatch in pattern:

Ch 25. Work rows 1–3 of Picot Lace pattern, then rows 2–3 three times more. After light blocking, swatch should measure 4¾" wide by 4" tall.

pattern notes

This garment is worked from the shoulders down in three pieces.

SPECIAL STITCHES

V-ST: (Dc, ch-2, dc) all in st indicated.

TRIPLE PICOT (worked in ch-sp of V-st from row below): (Sc in next ch, ch 3) four times.

PICOT LACE PATTERN

Worked over a multiple of 11 sts + 4.

ROW 1: Sc in 4th ch from hook, ch 3, sc in next ch, ch 3, skip 3 ch, V-st in next ch, *ch 3, skip 3 ch, triple picot, skip 3 ch, V-st in next ch**; repeat from * to ** across until 6 ch remain, ch 3, skip 3 ch, sc in next ch, ch 3, sc in next ch, ch 1, hdc. Turn.

ROW 2: Ch 3, dc in hdc, *ch 3, triple picot in next ch-2-sp, V-st in 2nd of next 3 ch-3-sp**. Repeat from * to ** across end with ch 3, (sc, ch 3) four times in last ch-2-sp, skip ch-3, sc, ch-3, sc. In final turning ch-sp, (dc, ch 1, dc). Turn.

ROW 3: Ch 2. (Hdc, ch 3, sc) in ch-1-sp, ch 3, *V-st in 2nd of next 3 ch-3-sp, ch 3, triple picot in next ch-2-sp.** Repeat from * to ** to last triple picot of row below, end with V-st in 2nd of next ch-3-sp, ch 3, (sc, ch3 hdc) in turning ch-sp. Turn.

Repeat rows 2 and 3 for pattern.

BACK AND SLEEVES

Worked from the top down.

Ch 234 (245, 256, 267). Place marker after first 81 ch from one end and 81 ch from other end to mark side seams. Be sure to move marker up a row as you work.

Work in stitch pattern, rows 1–3 once, then repeat rows 2–3 6 times more, then work row 2.

FINAL SLEEVE ROW

Ch 1, sc in first ch-sp, *ch 5, sc in 2nd of next 3 picots, ch 5, sc in in next ch-2-sp, sc**. Repeat from * to ** 6 times more (at your side edge marker). Sleeves will now remain unworked.

Continue to work the back.

Ch 2, in same-ch-sp, continue as if on a row 3 to next marker, ending at marker as for end of row 3.

Continue for second sleeve: *Ch 5, sc in 2nd of next 3 picots, ch 5, sc in next ch-2-sp, sc**. Repeat from * to ** to end of row, ending with a sc in turning ch. Fasten off. Turn.

FINISH BACK

Reattach yarn to marker at side of body with a sl st and, beginning with row 2 of pattern, work in pattern until body measures 14" from underarm, ending with row 2 of pattern.

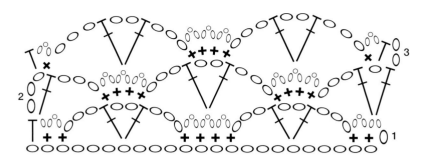

BACK EDGING

Ch 1, sc in first ch-sp, *ch 5, sc in 2nd of next 3 picots, ch 5, sc in in next ch-2-sp, sc**. Repeat from * to ** to end of row. Fasten off.

RIGHT SLEEVE AND RIGHT FRONT

With wrong side of back facing, attach yarn with a sl st to foundation row of sleeve at cuff. You will be working into the back side of the foundation ch. Beginning with row 1 of pattern, ch 3, sc in next ch, and continue across row as indicated until pattern has been worked over first 77 ch place stitch marker, then work over next 22 ch, ending as for end of row 1. Turn. Move marker every row to note beginning of right front.

Continue to work rows 2 and 3 until sleeve front is the same height as back sleeve, ending with row 2 of pattern.

FINAL ROW, RIGHT SLEEVE

Ch 1, sc in first ch-sp, *ch 5, sc in 2nd of next 3 picots, ch 5, sc in in next ch-2-sp, sc**. Repeat from * to ** to side edge, continue across front as for row 3.

BEGIN INCREASES FOR NECKLINE

INCREASE PATTERN

ROW 1: Ch 4, dc in hdc, continue as for row 2 of stitch pattern. Turn.

ROW 2: As for row 3 to last dc, (sc, ch3, sc, ch 3, hdc) in ch-4 at end of previous row. Turn.

ROW 3: Ch 5, dc in first ch-3-sp, continue as for row 2 of stitch pattern. Turn.

ROW 4: As for row 3 to last ch-5-sp, (sc, ch 3) 3 times in ch-5-sp, hdc in ch-5-sp. Turn.

ROW 5: Ch 4, V-st in 2nd of next 3 picots, continue as for row 2. Turn.

ROW 6: As for row 3 to last V-st, (sc, ch3) 4 times in ch-2-sp, dc in ch-4-sp. Turn.

ROW 7: Ch 4, dc in first dc, ch 3, skip V-st in 3rd of next 3 picots, continue as for row 2. Turn.

ROW 8: As for row 3 to last (dc, ch-4-sp), in ch-4-sp, work (dc, ch 1, dc). Turn.

ROW 9: (Ch 3, sc, ch 3, sc) in first ch-1-sp, continue as for row 2. Turn.

ROW 10: As for row 3 end with V-st in last picot. Turn.

ROW 11: Ch 4, (sc, ch 3, sc, ch 3, sc) in first ch-2-sp, continue as for row 2. Turn.

ROW 12: As for row 3 to last picot, in second to last picot, work V-st, ch 1, work dc in final ch-4-sp. Turn.

ROW 13: Ch 5, in next ch-2-sp, work (sc, ch 3) 4 times, continue as for row 2. Turn.

ROW 14: As for row 3 to last ch-5-sp, work (ch 3, sc, ch 3, hdc) in turning ch-5-sp. Turn.

FOR RIGHT SIDE ONLY

Work increase rows 1–14 twice, then rows 1–3, then add finishing row as for back. Fasten off.

LEFT SLEEVE AND LEFT FRONT

Skip first 6 ch-sp from right shoulder and attach yarn in center of next picot cluster with a sl st.

Beginning with row 1 of Picot Lace pattern, continue with sleeve until same length as the back sleeve.

On next row, continue in pattern until reaching back underarm, then add finishing as for right sleeve. Break yarn.

Reattach yarn at side of front directly below last row at underarm, attaching to first dc with a sl st.

Work Increase Pattern rows 10–14, then rows 1–14, then rows 1–12. Add finishing row. Cut yarn, and fasten off.

FINISHING

Lightly steam block. Sew side and underarm seams. Weave in ends.

TIES

Attach yarn with a sl st to position on front opening edge. Ch 30, turn, and sl st back into each ch. Repeat for opposite side.

DEEPEST PICOT CARDIGAN SCHEMATIC

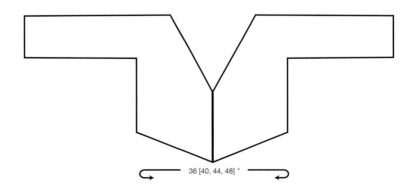

36 [40, 44, 48] "

charmed
TOP

debora oese-lloyd

This flirty top is created from a radiant bamboo yarn that shimmers across your fingers as you crochet. The hand-dyed yarn creates a subtle movement of blue tones like moonlight on lake water. The playful contrast of the solid bodice and the peekaboo lace skirt gives this top a "naughty-but-nice" look. Wear it alone or over a cami—either way, you'll look suitable for a romantic lakeside dinner.

SIZES

XS (S, M, L)

FINISHED MEASUREMENTS

CHEST: 30 (34, 38, 42)"

YARN

Alchemy Bamboo (100% bamboo; 150yds/50g): 8 (9, 9, 10) skeins, Moonstone (92w)

SUBSTITUTION: Approximately 1093 (1250, 1300, 1470) yds DK-weight yarn. Look for yarn that knits to 22–24 sts/4".

HOOKS

US C/2.75mm crochet hook, or size needed to obtain proper gauge

NOTIONS

Yarn needle

Three ⅝" buttons

2½ yds 1" white satin ribbon (optional)

GAUGE

Wattle Stitch (bodice): 11 clusters and 20 rows to 4"

Open Fan Stitch (skirt): 4 fans and 5 rows of fans to 4", unblocked; 3 fans and 4 rows of fans to 4", blocked

pattern notes

For best fit, choose a size slightly smaller than your actual bust measurement.

The Wattle Stitch bodice is worked back and forth in rows in 3 separate pieces (left and right front and the back). The upper bodice is sewn together before the lower bodice skirt is worked in the round in the Open Fan stitch.

Debora Oese-Lloyd lives in Calgary with her very devoted husband, Patrick. He does all the cooking and errand running so that she has more time to knit, crochet, and contemplate the mysteries of the universe. She is currently working with the statement, "The stillness is the dance," both in her knitting and her life.

SPECIAL STITCHES

CL (CLUSTER FOR WATTLE STITCH): (1 sc, ch 1, 1 dc)

STITCH PATTERNS

The following stitch pattern instructions are for the gauge swatches.

Please note that the Open Fan gauge swatch is worked back and forth in rows. The instructions for the top are written up in rounds because the skirt is worked in the round and the row connections vary slightly.

WATTLE STITCH

Ch 34.

ROW 1: Skip 2 ch (count as 1 sc) *work (1 sc, ch 1, 1 dc) into next chain, skip 2 ch*; repeat from * 11 times ending with 1 sc into turning ch, turn.

ROW 2: Ch 1 (count as 1 sc), skip first sc and next dc, *work (1 sc, ch 1, 1 dc) into next ch-1-sp, skip 1 sc and 1 dc*; repeat from * 10 times, ending with (1sc, ch 1, 1dc) into last ch-1-sp, skip next sc, 1 sc into top of turning ch, turn.

Repeat row 2.

OPEN FAN STITCH

Ch 37.

ROW 1: 1 sc into second ch from the hook, *ch 1, skip 4 ch into next chain work a fan of 1 tr (ch 2, 1 tr) 4 times, then ch 1, skip 4 ch, 1 sc into next chain*; repeat from * 3 times to last 5 ch, ch 1, skip 4 ch, into last ch work (1 tr, ch 2) twice and 1 tr, turn.

ROW 2: Ch 1, 1 sc into first st, *ch 3, skip next ch-2-sp, 1 dc into next sp**, ch 2, skip next tr, sc and tr and work 1 dc into ch-2-sp of next fan, ch 3, work 1 sc into center tr of fan; repeat from * ending last repeat at **, ch 1, 1 tr into last sc, skip turning ch, turn.

ROW 3: 7 ch (count as 1 tr and ch 2), skip first tr, work (1 tr, ch 2, 1 tr) into next ch-1-sp. Ch 1, skip ch-3-sp, 1 sc into next sc, *ch 1, skip next ch-3-sp, work a fan into next ch-2-sp, ch 1, skip next ch-3-sp, 1 sc into next sc, repeat from * to end, skip turning ch, turn.

ROW 4: 6 ch (count as 1 tr and 1 ch), skip first tr, work 1 dc into next ch-2-sp, ch 3, 1 sc into center tr of fan, *ch 3, skip next ch-2-sp, 1 dc, into next ch-2-sp, ch 2, skip next tr, sc, tr, work 1 dc into next ch-2-sp, ch 3, 1 sc into center tr of fan*; repeat from * ending last repeat in 3rd ch of turning ch, turn.

OPEN FAN STITCH

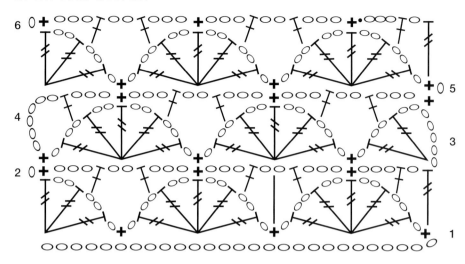

WATTLE STITCH

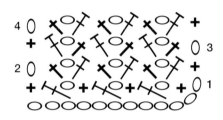

ROW 5: Ch 1, *1 sc into sc, ch 1, skip next ch-3-sp, fan into next ch-2-sp, ch 1, skip next ch-3-sp*; repeat from * to last sc, 1 sc into sc, ch 1, skip next ch-3-sp, work (1 tr, ch 2) twice and tr all into top of turning ch, turn.

Repeat rows 2–5.

BACK

Ch 114 (129, 147, 162).

ROW 1: Skip 2 ch (count as 1 sc) *work 1 cl into next chain, skip 2 ch; repeat from * 37 (42, 48, 53) times, ending with 1 sc into turning ch, turn.

ROW 2: Ch 1 (counts as 1 sc), skip first sc and next dc, *work 1 cl into ch-1-sp, skip 1 sc and 1 dc; repeat from * 36 (41, 47, 52) times, ending with 1 cl into last ch-1-sp. Skip next sc, 1 sc into turning ch, turn.

ROWS 3–8: Repeat row 2 6 (6, 6, 8) more times. On the last row ch 3 before turning.

ROW 9 (9, 9, 11): Skip 2 ch, work 1 cl into next chain, *work 1 cl into next ch-1-sp, skip 1 sc and 1 dc*; repeat from * 37 (42, 48, 53) times, sc in turning ch, ch 3 before turning.

ROW 10 (10, 10, 12): Skip 2 ch, work 1 cl into next ch, *work 1 cl into next ch-1-sp, skip 1 sc and 1 dc; repeat from * 37 (43, 48, 53) times ending with 1 cl into last ch-1-sp, skip next sc, 1 sc into turning ch, turn—total of 39 (44, 50, 55) clusters.

Repeat instruction for row 2 4 more times, incorporating the two new cls on the last row ch 3 before turning.

ROW 15 (15, 15, 17): Skip first 2 ch and work 1 cl into next ch, *work 1 cl into next ch-1-sp, skip 1 sc and 1 dc*; repeat from * 39 (44, 50, 55) times, 1 sc into last turning ch, ch 3 before turning.

ROW 16 (16, 16, 18): Skip 2 ch, work 1 cl into next ch, *work 1 cl into next ch-1-sp, skip 1 sc and 1 dc*; repeat from * 40 (45, 51, 56) times, 1 sc into last turning ch—total of 41 (46, 52, 57) clusters.

Incorporating the two new cl(s), repeat row 2 for 12 more rows for all sizes.

ARMHOLE SHAPING

ROW 29 (29, 29, 31): *Ch 1, sl 6 (6, 9, 9) sts across the first 2 (2, 3, 3) clusters, ch 1, sc in the next ch-1-sp, then work 1 cl in each remaining ch-1-sp, 1 sc in turning ch, turn*—a total of 38 (43, 48, 53) clusters.

ROW 30 (30, 30, 32): Repeat previous row between *s—3 (3, 4, 4) more clusters decreased for a total of 35 (40, 44, 49) clusters.

ROW 31 (31, 31, 33): Ch 1, sc in first ch-1-sp, work 33 (38, 42, 47) clusters in next ch-1-sps, 1 sc in the last ch-1-sp, turn—33 (38, 42, 47) clusters.

ROW 32 (32, 32, 34): Work as row 2 with 1 cl in each ch-1-sp.

SIZES XS, S, L ONLY

ROW 33 (33, 33, 35): Dec 1 cl on each side as described in Row 31.

SIZE M ONLY

Work as row 2 with 1 cl in each ch-1-sp—31 (36, 42, 45) clusters.

ALL SIZES

ROW 34 (34, 34, 36): Dec 1 cl on each side as described in row 31 (for sizes S and M) and row 33 (for size L).

SIZE XS ONLY

No decreases, work as established—31 (36, 40, 43) clusters.

ALL SIZES

Continue working with no further shaping on the armhole side only until row 44 (43, 42, 45). At the same time follow work the decreases for the neckline. The changes for the armhole decreases are included in the following sections. Follow the specific instructions for your size only.

SIZE XS ONLY

RIGHT BACK STRAP

ROW 36: Ch 1, 11 cl in first 11 ch-1-sp, 1 sc in 12th ch-1-sp, turn, leaving left back strap unworked until right side is complete.

ROW 37: Ch 1, skip first sc, 11 cl in ch-1-sp, sc in turning ch, turn.

ROW 38: Ch 1, 10 cl, sc in next ch-1-sp, turn.

ROW 39: Ch 1, 1 sc in first ch-1-sp, 9 cl. Sc in turning ch, turn.

ROW 40: Ch 1, 9 cl, 1 sc in next sc, turn.

ROW 41: Ch 1, sc in first ch-1-sp, 8 cl, sc in turning ch, turn.

ROW 42–43: Ch 1, 8 cl, sc in turning ch, turn.

ROW 44: Ch 1, sc in first ch-1-sp, 7 cl, sc in turning ch, turn.

ROWS 45–53: Ch 1, 7 cl, sc in turning ch, turn.

ROW 54: Ch 1, sc in first ch-1-sp, 6 cl, sc in turning ch, turn.

ROWS 55–58: Ch 1, 6 cl, sc in turning ch, turn.

ROW 59: Ch 1, 3cl, sc in next ch-1-sp, 6 sl sts to the end. Fasten off yarn.

LEFT BACK STRAP

Fasten yarn to the 20th cl from the right-hand edge. Ch 1 (counts as sc), 11 cl, sc in turning ch.

Continue as with the right back, reverse the shaping.

SIZE S ONLY

RIGHT BACK STRAP

ROW 36: Ch 1, 13 cl, sc in next ch-1-sp, turn. Leave the left back strap unworked until the right side is complete.

ROW 37: Ch 1, sc in first ch-1-sp 12 cl, sc in turning ch, turn.

ROW 38: Ch 1, 12 cl, sc in turning ch, turn.

ROW 39: Ch 1, sc in first ch-1-sp, 11 cl, sc in turning ch, turn.

ROW 40: Ch 1, 11 cl, sc in turning ch, turn.

ROW 41: Ch 1, sc in first ch-1-sp, 10 cl, sc in turning ch, turn.

ROWS 42–43: Ch 1, 10 cl, sc in turning ch, turn.

ROW 44: Ch 1, sc in first ch-1-sp, 9 cl, sc in turning ch, turn.

ROW 45: Ch 1, skip first sc, 8 cl in the ch-1-spaces, sc in turning ch, turn.

ROWS 46–54: Ch 1, 8 cl, sc in turning ch, turn.

ROW 55: Ch 1, 7 cl, sc in last ch-1-sp, turn.

ROW 56: Ch 1, skip first sc, 7 cl, sc in turning ch, turn.

ROWS 57–60: Ch 1, 7 cl, sc in turning ch, turn.

ROW 61: Ch 1, 4 cl, sc in 5th ch-1-sp, 9 sl sts across last 3 cl. Fasten off.

LEFT BACK STRAP

Attach yarn to the 23rd cl from the right-hand side edge, ch 1 (counts as sc), work 13 cl, sc into turning ch. Continue as with the right back, reverse the shaping for the neckline and armhole edges.

SIZE M ONLY

RIGHT BACK

ROW 38: Ch 1, work 14 cl, sc into the 15th cl from the right edge, turn, work only on the right back strap. You will reattach yarn to left side when the right back is complete.

ROWS 39–40: Ch 1, 14 cl, sc in turning ch, turn.

ROW 41: Ch 1, sc in first ch-1-sp, work 13 cl, sc in turning ch, turn.

ROW 42: Ch 1, 13 cl, sc in turning ch, turn.

ROW 43: Ch 1, sc in first ch-1-sp, work 12 cl, sc in turning ch, turn.

ROW 44: Ch 1, sc in first ch-1-sp, 11 cl, sc in last sc, turn.

ROWS 45–46: Ch 1, 11 cl, sc in last sc, turn.

ROW 47: Ch 1, sc in first ch-1-sp, work 10 cl, sc in turning ch, turn.

ROW 48: Ch 1, sc in first ch-1-sp, 9 cl sc in turning ch.

ROWS 49–55: Ch 1, 9 cl, sc in turning ch, turn.

ROW 56: Ch 1, 8 cl, sc in last ch-1-sp, turn.

ROWS 57–63: Ch 1, 8 cl, sc in turning ch, turn.

ROW 64: Ch 1, 9 sl sts over the first 3 cl, sc in 4th ch-1-sp, 4 cl. Fasten off yarn.

Attach yarn to the 26th cl from the right-hand side edge, ch 1 (counts as sc), work 14 cl, sc into turning ch. Continue as with the right back, reverse the shaping for the neckline and armhole edges.

SIZE L ONLY

RIGHT BACK

ROW 42: Ch 1, 15 cl, sc in next ch-1-sp (16th cl from right-hand side), turn, work only on the right back strap. You will reattach yarn to left side when the right back is complete.

ROW 43: Ch 1, sc in first ch-1-sp, 14 cl, sc in turning ch, turn.

ROW 44: Ch 1, sc in first ch-1-sp, 13 cl, sc in last sc, turn.

ROW 45: Ch 1, sc in first ch-1-sp, 12 cl, sc in last sc, turn.

ROWS 46–47: Ch 1, 12 cl, sc in last sc, turn.

ROW 48: Ch 1, 11 cl, sc in last ch-1-sp, turn.

ROWS 49–50: Ch 1, 11 cl, sc in last sc, turn.

ROW 51: Ch 1, sc in first ch-1-sp, 10 cl, sc in turning ch, turn.

ROWS 52–58: Ch 1, 10 cl, sc in turning ch, turn.

ROW 59: Ch 1, 9 cl, sc in ch-1-sp, turn.

ROWS 60–66: Ch 1, 9 cl, sc in turning ch, turn.

ROW 67: Ch 1, 5 cl, sc in next ch-1-sp, 9 sl sts over remaining 3 cl. Fasten off yarn.

Attach yarn to the 28th cl from the right-hand side edge, ch 1 (counts as sc), work 15 cl, sc into turning ch. Continue as with the right back, reverse the shaping for the neckline and armhole edges.

RIGHT FRONT

ALL SIZES

Ch 60 (69, 78, 87).

ROW 1: Skip 2 ch (count as 1 sc), *work (1 sc, ch 1, 1dc) into next ch, skip 2 ch*; repeat from * 19 (22, 25, 28) times, ending 1 sc into last ch, turn.

ROW 2: Ch 1, skip first sc and next dc work into each ch-1-sp, 1 sc into turning ch, turn.

Repeat row 2 6 (6, 6, 8) more times—19 (22, 25, 28) clusters across each row. Ch 3 at the end of the last row.

ROW 9 (9, 9, 11): Skip 2 ch, work 1 cl into next ch, work 1 cl into each ch-1-sp, sc into turning ch, ch 3, turn. This is an increase of 1 cl on the right side.

ROW 10 (10, 10, 12)–14 (14, 14, 16): Ch 1, 20 (23, 26, 29) cl, sc into turning ch. Work ch 3 at the end of the last row, turn.

ROW 15 (15, 15, 17): Repeat row 9 (9, 9, 11), turn, an increase of one cl on the right side—21 (24, 27, 30) cl.

ROW 16 (16, 16, 18)–28 (28, 28, 30): Ch 1, 21 (24, 27, 30) cl, sc in turning ch, turn.

BEGIN ARMHOLE SHAPING

ROW 29 (29, 29, 31): Ch 1, sl 6 (6, 9, 9) sts across 2 (2, 3, 3) cl, ch 1, sc in next ch-1-sp, then 18 (21, 23, 26) cl in remaining ch-1-sp across the row, sc in turning ch, turn.

ROW 30 (30, 30, 32): Ch 1, 18 (21, 23, 26) cl, sc in turning ch, turn.

SIZES XS, S, M ONLY

Size L begin separate instructions below.

ROW 31 (31, 31): Ch 1, sc in first ch-1-sp, 17 (20, 22) cl, sc in turning ch, turn.

ROW 32: Ch 1, 17 (20, 22) cl, sc in turning ch, turn.

Sizes XS, S, M begin separate instructions below.

RIGHT FRONT (CONT.)

SIZE XS ONLY

ROW 33: Ch 1, sc in first ch-1-sp, 13 cl, sc in next ch-1-sp, leave remaining 2 cl unworked, turn.

ROW 34: Ch 1, skip first sc, sc in first ch-1-sp, 12 cl, sc in turning ch, turn.

ROW 35: Ch 1, 11 cl, sc in last ch-1-sp, turn

ROW 36: Ch 1, skip first sc sc in first ch-1-sp, 10 cl, sc in turning ch, turn.

ROW 37: Ch 1, 10 cl, sc in turning ch, turn.

ROW 38: Ch 1, sc in first ch-1-sp, 9 cl, sc in turning ch, turn.

ROW 39: Ch 1, 9 cl, sc in turning ch, turn.

ROW 40: Ch 1, sc in first ch-1-sp, 8 cl, sc in turning ch, turn.

ROWS 41–43: Ch 1, 8 cl, sc in turning ch, turn.

ROW 44: Ch 1, 7 cl, sc in last ch-1-sp, turn.

ROWS 45–53: Ch 1, 7 cl, sc in turning ch, turn.

ROW 54: Ch 1, 6 cl, sc in last ch-1-sp, turn.

ROWS 55–58: Ch 1, 6 cl, sc in turning ch, turn.

ROW 59: Ch 1, 6 sl st across the first 2 cl, sc in next ch-1-sp, 3 cl. Fasten off.

LEFT FRONT BODICE

Complete as for the right front bodice, reversing the armhole and neckline shaping.

RIGHT FRONT (CONT.)

SIZE S ONLY

ROW 33: Ch 1, sc in first ch-1-sp, 16 cl, sc in next ch-1-sp, leaving 2 cl unworked, turn.

ROW 34: Ch 1, skip first sc, sc in first ch-1-sp, 15 cl, sc in turning ch, turn.

ROW 35: Ch 1, 14 cl, sc in last ch-1-sp, turn.

ROW 36: Ch 1, skip first sc, sc in first ch-1-sp, 13 cl, sc in turning ch, turn.

ROW 37: Ch 1, 12 cl, sc in last ch-1-sp, turn.

ROW 38: Ch 1, skip first sc, 12 cl, sc in turning ch, turn.

ROW 39: Ch 1, 11 cl, sc in last ch-1-sp, turn.

ROW 40: Ch 1, 11 cl, sc in turning ch, turn.

ROW 41: Ch 1, 10 cl, sc in last ch-1-sp, turn.

ROW 42: Ch 1, skip first sc, 10 cl, sc in turning ch, turn.

ROW 43: Ch 1, sc in first ch-1-sp, 9 cl, sc in turning ch, turn.

ROW 44: Ch 1, 9 cl, sc in turning ch, turn.

ROW 45: Ch 1, sc in first ch-1-sp, 8 cl, sc in turning ch, turn.

ROWS 46–54: Ch 1, 8 cl, sc in turning ch, turn.

ROW 55: Ch 1, sc in first ch-1-sp, 7 cl, sc in turning ch.

ROWS 56–60: Ch 1, 7 cl, sc in turning ch, turn.

ROW 61: 6 sl sts over first 2 cl, sc in next ch-1-sp, 4 cl. Fasten off yarn.

LEFT FRONT BODICE

Complete as for the right front bodice, reversing the armhole and neckline shaping.

RIGHT FRONT BODICE (CONT.)

SIZE M ONLY

ROW 33: Ch 1, 22 cl, sc in turning ch, turn.

ROW 34: Ch 1, 21 cl, sc in last ch-1-sp, turn.

ROW 35: Ch 1, 17 cl, sc into next ch-1-sp, turn leaving 3 cl unworked.

ROW 36: Ch 1, skip the first sc, 17 cl, sc in turning ch, turn.

ROW 37: Ch 1, 15 cl, sc in next ch-1-sp, turn.

ROW 38: Ch 1, skip the first sc, 15 cl, sc in turning ch, turn.

ROW 39: Ch 1, 14 cl, sc in last ch-1-sp, turn.

ROW 40: Ch 1, skip first sc, 13 cl, sc in turning ch, turn.

ROW 41: Ch 1, 12 cl, sc in last ch-1-sp, turn.

ROW 42: Ch 1, skip the first sc, 12 cl, sc in turning ch, turn.

ROW 43: Ch 1, sc in first ch-1-sp, 10 cl, sc in last ch-1-sp, turn.

ROWS 44–47: Ch 1, 10 cl, sc in turning ch, turn.

ROW 48: Ch 1, 9 cl, sc in last ch-1-sp, turn.

ROWS 49–55: Ch 1, 9 cl, sc in turning ch, turn.

ROW 56: Ch 1, 8 cl, sc in last ch-1-sp, turn.

ROW 57–63: Ch 1, 8 cl, sc in turning ch, turn.

ROW 63: Ch 1, 4 cl, sc in next ch-1-sp, 9 sl sts across remaining 3 cl. Fasten off yarn.

LEFT FRONT BODICE

Complete as for the right front bodice, reversing the armhole and neckline shaping.

RIGHT FRONT BODICE (CONT.)

SIZE L ONLY

ROW 33: Ch 1, 26 cl, sc in turning ch, turn.

ROW 34: Ch 1, 25 cl, sc in last ch-1-sp, turn.

ROW 35: Ch 1, 25 cl, sc in turning ch, turn.

ROW 36: Ch 1, 24 cl, sc in last ch-1-sp, turn.

ROW 37: Ch 1, sc in first ch-1-sp, 23 cl, sc in turning ch, turn.

ROWS 38–39: Ch 1, 23 cl, sc in turning ch, turn.

ROW 40 (BEGINS NECKLINE): 9 sl sts across first 3 cl, sc in next ch-1-sp, 19 cl leaving 3 cl unworked, sc in turning ch, turn.

ROW 41: Ch 1, 16 cl, sc in next ch-1-sp leaving 2 cl unworked, turn.

ROW 42: Ch 1, skip the first sc, sc in first ch-1-sp, 15 cl, sc in turning ch, turn.

ROW 43: Ch 1, 14 cl, sc in last ch-1-sp, turn.

ROW 44: Ch 1, skip first sc, sc in first ch-1-sp, 13 cl, sc in turning ch, turn.

ROW 45: Ch 1, sc in first ch-1-sp, 11 cl, sc in last ch-1-sp, turn.

ROW 46: Ch 1, skip first sc, sc in first ch-1-sp, 10 cl, sc in last sc, turn.

ROWS 47–59: Ch 1, 10 cl, sc in turning ch, turn.

ROW 60: Ch 1, 9 cl, sc in last ch-1-sp, turn.

ROW 61: Ch 1, skip first sc, 9 cl, sc in turning ch, turn.

ROWS 62–67: Ch 1, 9 cl, sc in turning ch, turn.

ROW 68: Ch 1, 5 cl, sc in next ch-1-sp, 9 sl st over last 3 cl. Fasten off yarn.

LEFT FRONT BODICE

Complete as for the right front bodice, reversing the armhole and neckline shaping.

PREPARING THE BODICE FOR WORKING THE SKIRT IN THE ROUND

FOR ALL SIZES

Steam block all three pieces of the bodice, using the schematic as a sizing guide. Use a press cloth and steam iron on medium heat.

BODICE CENTER FRONT EDGING AND BUTTONHOLES

LEFT FRONT: Attach yarn to bottom corner and work 38 (40, 42, 46) sc crochet along the left front center edge. Fasten off yarn.

RIGHT FRONT EDGE (BUTTONHOLES): Attach yarn to the upper neckline corner. Work 3 sc, 4 ch, 10 (11, 12, 14) sc, 4 ch, 10 (11, 12, 14) sc, 4 ch, 3 sc along the center front edge, turn.

Work 38 (40, 42, 46) sc into both the sc and ch sts of the previous row. Fasten off yarn.

SIDE AND SHOULDER SEAMS, ALL SIZES

Sew together the side and shoulder seams with ¼" seams. Overlap the right front bodice over the left front bodice ½" and stitch in place at the lower edge.

LOWER BODICE SKIRT

ALL SIZES

With the right side facing you, attach your yarn to the right side seam. Work 80 (85, 90, 100) sc across the lower front edge of the bodice and 80 (85, 90, 100) sc across the lower back bodice edge.

BEGIN OPEN FAN STITCH IN THE ROUND

Note that the connection between rounds is different than the back and forth instruction of the gauge swatch.

ROUND 1: Ch 1 (count as sc) *ch 1, skip 4 sc, into next sc work a fan of 1 tr (ch 2, 1 tr) 4 times, then ch 1, skip 4 sc, 1 sc into next sc, repeat from * 17 (18, 19, 21) times, sl st into starting ch 1. Do not turn.

ROUND 2: Sl st along the first fan until you are at the ch-2-sp between the 1st and 2nd tr.

6 ch (counts as 1 dc and ch 3), sc into top of middle tr, ch 3, skip next ch-2-sp, dc into following ch-2-sp, *ch 2, work 1 dc into first ch-2-sp of next fan, ch 3, sc in to middle tr, ch 3, skip next ch-2-sp and dc into the following ch-2-sp of the fan, repeat from * to the end of the round, ch 2 and sl st into 3rd chain of the starting 6 ch at the start of the round. Turn.

ROUND 3: You will now work 2 sl sts going backwards until you are in the ch-2-sp you just worked at the end of the previous round. Turn your work again, you should now have the right side facing you. 7 ch (counts as 1 tr and ch 2), work 1 tr (ch 2, 1 tr) 3 times into the same ch-2-sp that the 7 ch is located in, ch 1, *sc in the sc over the middle tr of the previous fan row, ch 1, work tr (ch 2, tr) 4 times into the next ch-2-sp, ch 1, repeat from * to the end of the round. Sl st into 5th ch of the starting 7 ch, begin round 2—17 (18, 19, 21) fans worked.

Note that the end of the round will move back one fan every other row because of this slip stitching backwards.

Repeat rounds 2–3 4 (5, 5, 6) more times.

ROUND 12 (14, 14, 16): In this increase round you will work 2 fans at each of the sides where you would normally work only 1 fan. This is the set-up row for working the extra fans in the next row.

Sl st to the ch-2-sp between the 1st and 2nd tr, 6 ch, sc into of middle tr, ch 3, skip next ch-2-sp, dc into next ch-2-sp, *ch 2, work 1dc into first ch-2-sp of next fan, ch 3, sc into to of middle tr, ch 3, skip next ch-2-sp, dc into next ch-2-sp of fan, repeat from * until you are at the valley between 2 fans that lines up most closely to the side seams then follow the instructions between the **. You are working 2 ch-2-sp here instead of the established patterns on ch-2-sp. In the fan to the right of the

seam work the usual dc in ch-2-sp between 1st and 2nd tr, ch 3, sc above middle tr, ch 3, skip next ch-2-sp, dc in next ch-2-sp. Now work ch 2 and instead of moving on to the next fan work a dc in the sc between fans, ch 2 and continue on to the next fan as established in the pattern** and repeat at between ** at the other side seam. Complete the round in the established pattern. (See illustration.)

ROUND 13 (15, 15, 17): Work round 3 incorporating the 2 extra fans—19 (20, 21, 23) fans.

Repeat rounds 2 and 3 once more.

ROUND 16 (18, 18, 20): This is another increase row. This time you will set up for working 2 fans on either side of the fan that lines up with the side seams. There will be 4 more fans worked on the next round, two at each side.

Proceed with a round 2 and repeat the instructions between the ** of round 12 (14, 14, 16) in the valleys just before and just after the side seam fan.

ROUND 17 (19, 19, 21): Repeat round 3, working 2 fans in the valley on either side of the side seam fan—23 (24, 25, 27) fans.

Repeat rounds 2 and 3 once more.

ROUND 20 (22, 22, 24): This row is similar to round 2 but it is a set-up row for making larger fans (6 tr instead of 5 tr) in the following row. Simply work ch 3 between the dc instead of the established ch 2.

Sl st to first ch-2-sp, ch 7 (instead of 6), sc in sc over middle tr, ch 3, skip next ch-2-sp, dc in next ch-2-sp, ch 3, *dc in first ch-2-sp next fan, ch 3, sc over middle tr, ch 3, skip next ch-2-sp, dc in next ch-2-sp, ch 3, repeat from * to the end of the round.

ROUND 21 (23, 23, 25): Turn your work and sl st back to the last ch-3-sp of the previous round, turn your work again, 7 ch (count as 1 tr and ch 2), tr (ch 2, 1 tr) 4 times, ch 1, sc over middle tr of previous fan round, ch 1, *tr (ch 2, tr) 5 times, ch 1, sc over middle tr of previous fan round, ch 1, repeat from * to the end of round.

ROUND 22 (24, 24, 26): Sc edging. Sl st into 5th ch of starting 7 ch, ch 1, 1 sc in each tr and 2 sc in each ch-2-sp, skip ch-1-sp, sc in sc between fans, work across the round and sl st into 1st ch 1. Fasten off.

FINISHING

Work a row of sc along both the armholes and the neckline. Then work the following edgings:

NECKLINE

ROW 1: Attach yarn to right front bodice corner, ch 1, work 40 (44, 48, 52) sc along right front bodice neck edge, 80 (84, 92, 100) sc along the back neck edge, and 40 (44, 48, 52) sc along the left front bodice neck edge, turn.

ROW 2 (SCALLOP EDGING): Ch 1, skip 1st sc, 3 dc in next sc, skip next sc, sc in next sc, *skip next sc, 3 dc in next sc, skip next sc, sc in next sc, repeat from * across entire neckline, fasten off yarn—10 (11, 12, 13) scallops on left and right front edge, 20 (21, 23, 25) scallops across back neck edge.

ARMHOLES

ROUND 1: Attach yarn to underarm side seam, ch 1, work 92 (96, 100, 108) sc around edge, sl st into 1st ch 1—23 (24, 25, 27) scallops.

ROUND 2: Ch 1, * skip 1 sc, 3 dc in next sc, skip 1 sc, sc in next sc, repeat aound the armhole, sl st into 1st ch 1. Fasten off yarn.

Use a tapestry needle to weave in all ends.

Steam block the skirt with iron on a medium setting and using a pressing cloth. Use the schematic as a guide for shaping.

Sew buttons on to the left front bodice in line with the button loops.

LOOPS FOR RIBBON (OPTIONAL)

Attach yarn at the side seams and at the center front. Work an 8 ch loop, attach them 1" above lower bodice seam.

CHARMED TOP SCHEMATIC

6.5 [7, 7, 7.5] "

30 [34, 38, 42] "

36 [38, 40, 43] "

CHAPTER TWO

DARE TO BARE

flaunt it with these stunning tops

red hot
HALTER

amy swenson

SIZES

XS (S, M, L, XL, 2X)

FINISHED MEASUREMENTS

CHEST: 30 (34, 38, 40, 44, 48)"

YARN

Alchemy Silk Purse (100% silk; 163yds/50g): 4 (4, 5, 5, 6) skeins, Poppy

SUBSTITUTION: Approximately 525 (595, 665, 770, 840) yds DK-weight yarn. Look for yarn that knits to 22–24 sts/4".

HOOKS

US B/2.25mm crochet hook, or size needed to obtain proper gauge

NOTIONS

Yarn needle

2 yds 1"-wide grosgrain ribbon, shown in black

GAUGE

20 sc to 4"

A triangle-shaped halter top is universally flattering. This one features a feminine flair, by way of a "naughty but nice" black ribbon finish. Worked in a luscious pure silk and the simplest of stitches, the fabric created is structured yet sensual. Wear this one with a sleek skirt or fashionable pants, alone or layered under a jacket or shrug. In any case, you'll turn heads.

pattern notes

This pattern is designed to fit A–C cups best. To adjust for a larger cup size, when beginning the triangle shaping, work additional stitches, creating a 1–3" crossover of the triangle fabric at the center front. Decrease as indicated. This will make larger triangles, and the overlap will allow for better support.

RIBBON BAND

This band is worked side to side, and should measure 2" wide.

Ch 11.

ROW 1: Sc in 2nd and each ch across; 10 sc, turn.

ROWS 2–10: Ch 1, sc in 1st st and each st across; 10 sc, turn.

ROW 11: Ch 3, dc in 1st sc, ch 6, skip 6 sc, dc in last 2 sc, turn.

ROW 12: Ch 1, sc in 1st 2 dc, 6 sc in ch-6-sp, sc in last dc and turning ch; 10 sc.

Work rows 1–12 a total of 12 (14, 16, 18, 20, 22) times. Fasten off.

Sew chain edge to last row to join the band.

FIRST CUP

Position band so seam is at the center of the back. Lay band on a flat surface with front right side facing. Using scrap yarn or removable stitch markers, mark 2 new "side seam" stitches. Each marker should be at the center side points of the band.

With right side of work facing and beginning at left side seam marker, attach yarn with sl st. Ch 1, sc 64 (74, 84, 94, 104, 114) sts evenly across top front of Ribbon Band, turn.

ROW 1: Ch 1, sc across all sc.

ROW 2: Split for triangle cup shaping as follows: Ch 1, sc across next 32 (37, 42, 47, 52, 57) sts, turn.

BEGIN CUP SHAPING

ROW 1: Ch 1, sc in 2nd sc and each across, (1 st dec).

Repeat row 1, dec 1 st at the begining of each row, until 3 sc remain.

STRAP

Work rows of sc over 3 sts until strap is 16" or desired length.

Cut yarn and secure.

SECOND CUP

Reattach yarn with a sl st, in middle front of camisole in same sc as first.

ROW 1: Ch 1, sc across remaining 32 (37, 42, 47, 52, 57) front sts.

Work cup shaping and strap as for first cup.

BODY

You'll now attach yarn to the bottom of the Ribbon Band and crochet the camisole down to the hem. The body is worked in a spiral fashion, so you will not be joining rounds.

With right side facing and begining at right side seam, attach yarn with a sl st.

Ch 1, work 64 (74, 84, 94, 104, 114) sc evenly across bottom front of Ribbon Band, then sc 64 (74, 84, 94, 104, 114) sts evenly across bottom back of Ribbon Band, sl st to initial sc and begin working in rounds over 128 (148, 168, 188, 208, 228) sts.

Work even rounds of sc for 5 inches. On next round, inc 1 st on both sides of each side seam—4 sts increased. Work 7 rounds even. Increase in this way every 8th round 3 times more—144 (164, 184, 204, 224, 244) sts total.

Continue even until body measures 8" from bottom of Ribbon Band, or to your desired length.

RED HOT HALTER SCHEMATIC

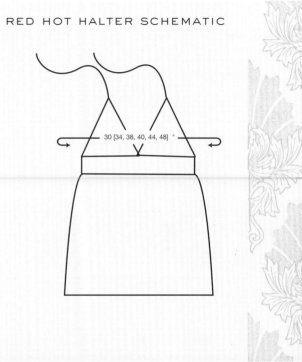

30 [34, 38, 40, 44, 48]

EDGING

Ch 3, skip first 3 sc, *dc in next sc, ch 3, 4 dc around stem of previous dc, skip next 3 sc**, repeat from * to ** ending with ch 3, skip 3 sc, sl st in begining of round.

Fasten off.

With sl st, reattach yarn to front center edge of cup. Work edging as above along inside edge of each cup.

With sl st, reattach yarn to outer edge of right cup, just below the strap. Sl st evenly down side of cup, across back of halter, and up along the outer edge of left cup. Fasten off.

FINISHING

Weave in ends.

Weave ribbon through holes on band with ends positioned at front of work as shown. Tie in a bow.

one-skein backless
HALTER

amy swenson

amy swenson

You know that perfect skein of hand-dyed cashmere you've been hoarding in your stash for far too long? This sexy top is my solution to stash satisfaction. Inspired by handkerchief halters, a large crocheted square is tied artfully at six places to show just the right amount of skin. The halter uses one skein for the smaller size and one- and-a-half for the larger size. Want a more summer-worthy top? Try it in a silk/cotton blend for a beach-ready feel.

pattern notes

The sizing on this halter is controlled by the size of the finished square. While crocheting, be sure to try it on from time to time. When the proper size is obtained, the width of the square will cover your breasts at the widest point.

The piece will not be a perfect square. Instead, the sides will pull in, leaving pointed corners at each of the ch-3-sp. This will ensure a correct fit.

SIZES

S–M (L–XL)

FINISHED MEASUREMENTS

WIDTH: 13 (16)"

YARN

Handmaiden 4-ply Cashmere (100% cashmere; 185yds/50g): 1 (2) skeins, Rose Garden

SUBSTITUTION: Approximately 186 (273) yds DK-weight yarn. Look for yarn that knits to 22-24 sts/4". For similar results, choose a cashmere or cashmere-blend yarn.

HOOKS

US E/3.5mm crochet hook, or size needed to obtain proper gauge

NOTIONS

Yarn needle

2 yd ½–⅝" ribbon, or create a crocheted chain to tie the halter

GAUGE

16 dc to 4"

SQUARE

Worked in joined rounds without turning.

ROUND 1: Ch 3. Do not join. Into 3rd ch from hook, work 2 dc, then (ch 3, 3 dc into ch) 3 times, ch 3, sl st to join to initial ch-3.

ROUND 2: Ch 3 (counts as 1 dc), work 1 dc into each dc, and (3 dc, ch 3, 3 dc) into each corner ch-3-sp. At end of round, join to initial ch-3 with a sl st.

Repeat round 2 12 (16) times, or until width of square fits properly across front of your chest. Fasten off.

FINISHING

Make side loops as follows (make one on each side): Attach yarn to center of side edge with a sl st, ch 6, sl st into same st where joined. Fasten off.

Weave in all ends. Wet block and let dry.

To wear, with wrong side facing, weave ribbon through right top corner ch-3-sp, down right side through the side loop, across to the lower left corner (through ch-3-sp), across the lower edge to the lower right corner (through ch-3-sp), up to left side loop, up the left side to the top left corner, then tie behind the neck. Spaces between top corners and side loops become armholes.

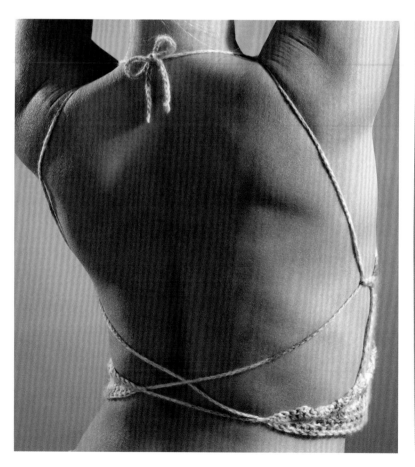

DARE TO BARE   67

strapless sage
CORSET

amy swenson

amy swenson

SIZES

XS (S, M, L, XL, 2X, 3X)

FINISHED MEASUREMENTS

CHEST: 29 (31, 33, 35, 37, 39, 41)"

YARN

RYC Cashcotton DK (35% cotton, 25% nylon, 18% angora, 13% rayon, 9% cashmere; 142yds/50g): 3 (3, 3, 3, 3, 3, 4) skeins, Sage

SUBSTITUTION: Approximately 284 (306, 328, 350, 372, 383, 437) yds DK-weight yarn. Look for yarn that knits to 22–24 sts/4". For best results choose a cotton or silk-blend yarn.

HOOKS

US G/4.0mm crochet hook, or size needed to obtain proper gauge

NOTIONS

Yarn needle

Removeable stitch markers

GAUGE

16 hdc to 4"

Summer needs a little luxury too! This corset-inspired strapless top uses a fabulous blend from Rowan Yarn Classics. "Cashcotton" combines the strength of cotton with angora and cashmere for a soft-against-the-skin sensation. Worked from the top edge to the hem, the solid bodice features gentle shaping for a great fit. Next, an easy and stylish mesh is worked to the desired length, then finished off with a solid hem.

pattern notes

For proper fit, choose a chest circumference 1 to 3" smaller than your actual bust measurements. Remember, this isn't your bra size! Instead, wrap a measuring tape around the widest part of your bust and use this to select the proper size.

SPECIAL STITCH

HDC3TOG (HALF DOUBLE CROCHET THREE TOGETHER): (yo, insert hook into next stitch and pull up a loop) three times; yo and pull through all 7 loops—2 stitches decreased

BUST

All rounds are joined with a sl st. Do not turn at the ends of rounds.

Ch 100 (108, 116, 124, 132, 140, 148), sl st to join.

ROUND 1: Ch 2, hdc evenly around, sl st to join.

BUST INCREASES

ROUND 2: Ch 2, work 15 hdc, in next stitch, work 3 hdc, place marker in center of 3 hdc, continue for 18 (20, 22, 24, 26, 28, 30) hdc, 3 hdc, place marker in center of 3 hdc in next stitch, continue around to end—4 stitches increased.

ROUND 3: Work even, move markers up to maintain position.

ROUND 4: Ch 2, hdc to marker, work 3 hdc in marked st, (move marker to center of 3 hdc) hdc to next marker, work 3 hdc in marked st, (move marker to center of 3 hdc), hdc to end of round—4 stitches increased.

ROUNDS 5–6: Repeat rounds 3–4.

ROUND 7: Repeat round 3.

ROUND 8: Ch 2, work 18 hdc, in next stitch, work 3 hdc, move 1st marker to the center st of increase, continue for 24 (26, 28, 30, 32, 34, 36) hdc, in next stitch, work 3 hdc, move 2nd marker st of increase, continue to end of round—4 stitches increased; 116 (124, 132, 140, 148, 156, 164) stitches total.

Work 6 (6, 7, 7, 8, 9, 10) rounds even, moving stitch markers up every round to maintain the position.

BUST DECREASES

ROUND 1: Work hdc to 1 st before marker, hdc3tog over next 3 sts, place marker in top of decrease, hdc to 1 stitch before second marker, hdc3tog over next 3 sts, place marker in top of decrease, hdc to end of round.

ROUND 2: Work even.

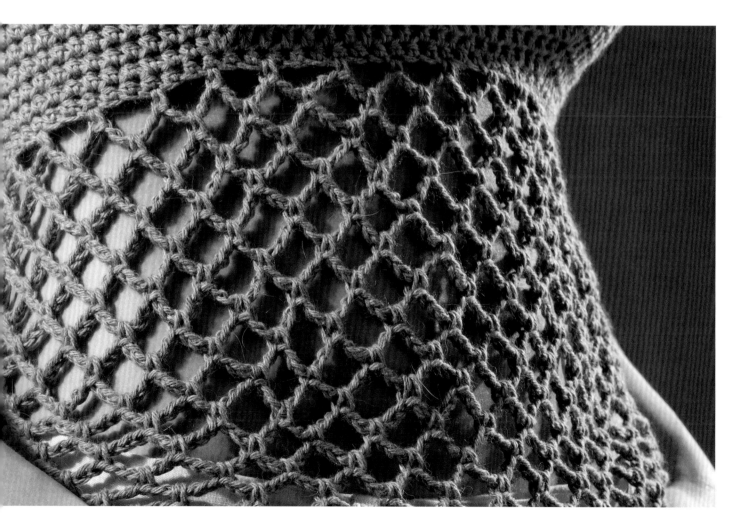

ROUNDS 3–6: Repeat rounds 1–2.

Fasten off. This edge forms the top edge of the corset.

BODICE

Worked in a spiral without turns or joining.

ROUND 1: With sl st, reattach yarn to bottom of foundation ch. (Ch 4, skip 2 hdc, sc in next hdc) to end of round, placing final sc in st next to sl st.

ROUND 2: (Ch 5, sc in ch-sp), repeat around. At end of round, do not join. Instead, continue by placing next sc in next ch-5-sp.

Continue until mesh portion measures 10 (10, 11, 11, 12, 12, 13)" from bottom of corset when slightly stretched.

Pull the mesh open at this point, as the unblocked length will be significantly shorter than the final length when the hem is finished and the piece is blocked.

HEM

Worked in joined rounds without turning.

ROUND 1: (Ch 3, sc in ch-sp) around. Sl st to join.

ROUND 2: Ch 2, work 3 hdc in each ch-sp around. Sl st to join.

ROUND 3: Ch 2, work hdc in each hdc around. Sl st to join.

Repeat last round once more. Sl st to join. Fasten off.

FINISHING

Sew in all ends.

Steam or wet block as desired.

SPAGHETTI STRAPS (OPTIONAL)

Attach yarn to top front of corset in desired position, using a sl st. Ch 30. Turn, sl st back into each ch to end. Cut yarn and sew in place. Repeat for other side of top. When finished, tie behind neck.

STRAPLESS SAGE CORSET SCHEMATIC

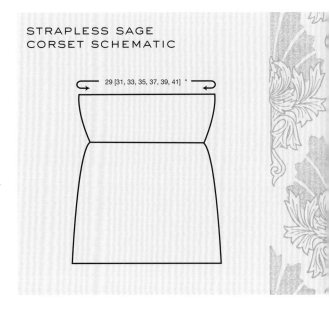

29 [31, 33, 35, 37, 39, 41] "

retro femme
EMPIRE WAIST

amy swenson

SIZES

XS (S, M, L, XL)

FINISHED MEASUREMENTS

CHEST: 34 (37, 40, 43, 45)"

YARN

Cascade Cloud 9 (50% wool, 50% angora; 109yds/50g): 4 (5, 6, 6) skeins, color 112

SUBSTITUTION: Approximately 405 (437, 514, 547) yds worsted-weight yarn. Look for yarn that knits to 18–20 sts/4". For best results, choose an angora-blend yarn.

HOOKS

US H/5.0mm crochet hook, or size needed to obtain proper gauge

NOTIONS

Yarn needle

Removeable stitch markers

GAUGE

14 sts and 6 rows of Pike Stitch equals 4" square

This angora-blend top is inspired by the sweetly romantic fashions of the '40s, with a modern flare. The waistline is emphasized by a seed stitch band, and two different extended single crochet stitch patterns highlight the top and bottom halves of the finished garment. A keyhole neckline provides more than a touch of sensuality. Be daring and wear this over bare skin, or choose a silk cami to layer underneath.

pattern notes

Due to the keyhole construction of this top, you'll obtain the best fit when selecting a finished chest size approximately ½" *smaller* than your actual chest measurements. As the stitch pattern is stretchy, err on the side of selecting a smaller size. Top is worked in one piece from the neck edge down.

SPECIAL STITCHES

EXSC (EXTENDED SINGLE CROCHET): insert hook into next stitch and pull up a loop, yo and pull through first loop, yo and pull through remaining 2 loops

PIKE STITCH PATTERN

Chain an odd number of sts plus 4.

ROW 1: Exsc in 5th ch from hook, *ch 1, skip 1 ch, exsc in next ch* to end of row.

ROW 2: Ch 3, skip (1 exsc 1 ch), *exsc in next exsc, ch 1, skip 1 ch* to end of row, exsc in turning ch.

Repeat row 2 for pattern.

NECK OPENING

Ch 75 (75, 85, 85, 85), work row 1 of Pike Stitch pattern.

RAGLAN INCREASES

You'll now place removable stitch markers to note position for raglan increases.

FOR SIZES XS AND S

Place markers in 7th, 11th, 26th and 30th ch-1-sp.

FOR SIZES M, L, AND XL

Place markers in 9th, 13th, 29th, and 33rd ch-1-sp.

ROW 1: *Work as for row 2 of Pike Stitch pattern to exsc before marker, (exsc, ch 1, exsc) in same st, ch 1, move marker up into this ch-1-sp, (exsc, ch 1, exsc) in exsc after marker**. Repeat from * to ** around four times around, finish row as for row 2 of Pike Stitch pattern—4 sets of raglan increases made.

ROWS 2–3: Repeat row 1.

Work even without increasing a total of 3 (4, 4, 4, 5) times.

FOR SIZES XS AND L ONLY

Repeat row 1.

ALL SIZES

Work 2 (0, 2, 2, 2) more rows without increasing.

You'll now split the front and the back and work each part separately.

RIGHT FRONT

Work in pattern to exsc before marked ch-sp. Exsc, turn.

Work 3 more rows of Pike Stitch pattern over just these stitches. Fasten off.

BACK

Skip over right sleeve sts and attach yarn to exsc after marker with sl st. Beginning with ch 3, work as for row 2 to exsc before next marker. Exsc in this st, turn.

Work 3 more rows of Pike Stitch pattern over just these stitches. Fasten off.

LEFT FRONT

Skip over left sleeve sts and attach yarn to exsc after marker with sl st. Beginning with ch 3, work as for row 2 to end of row. Work 3 more rows over just these stitches. Fasten off.

JOIN UNDERARMS

ROW 1: Beginning at right front edge, reattach yarn with a sl st. Work in pattern to underarm, ch 5 (5, 7, 7, 7), continue in pattern across back, ch 5 (5, 7, 7, 7) for left underarm, and continue in pattern across front.

ROW 2: On next row, continue in pattern as established, working into the underarm ch sts as necessary.

Work in stitch pattern for 6 more rows. Fasten off.

EMPIRE WAISTBAND

With right side facing, attach yarn at right side edge with sl st into exsc. (Ch 1, sc in ch-1-sp) to front edge, placing last sc in turning ch at edge. Ch 1, place next sc in 1st ch-sp of opposite front edge to join and work in rounds. Do not sl st. Continue to spiral without turning, working sc mesh (ch 1, sc in ch-1-sp) around until band measures 2".

WAIST

Worked in rounds spiraling without joining or turning.

ROUND 1: Ch 3, *skip 1 ch-sp, in next ch-sp (exsc, ch 2, exsc)**. Repeat from * to ** around, ending with exsc, ch 2 in initial sl st. Continue around until piece measures 13 (13, 14, 14, 15)" from underarm or desired length. When finishing final round, join with a sl st into final ch-2-sp.

FINISHING

Sew in all ends.

Sl st around arm openings and front edges.

Sew neck edge together at opening to create keyhole.

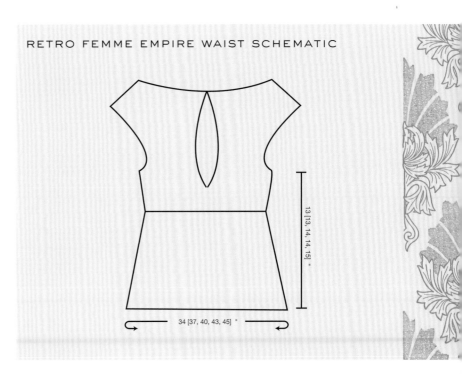

RETRO FEMME EMPIRE WAIST SCHEMATIC

13 [13, 14, 14, 15] "

34 [37, 40, 43, 45] "

plum thunder
CAMISOLE

amy swenson

SIZES

XS (S, M, L, XL, 2X, 3X)

FINISHED MEASUREMENTS

CHEST: 33 (35, 37, 39, 41, 43, 45)"

YARN

Curious Creek Oban (50% wool, 50% silk; 205yds/95g): 2 (3, 3, 3, 3, 4, 4) skeins, Plum Thunder

SUBSTITUTION: Approximately 427 (448, 492, 547, 601, 678, 765) yds aran-weight yarn. Look for yarn that knits to 18–20 sts/4".

HOOKS

US G/4.0mm crochet hook, or size needed to obtain proper gauge

NOTIONS

Yarn needle

GAUGE

1 French Square measures 4½" square after blocking.

Nothing showcases crochet more than an elegant stitch worked in a spectacular yarn. Here, I've adapted a traditional French Square motif to add a bit of texture down the front and back of this slinky camisole. Curious Creek's luxurious Oban silk/merino yarn in delicious shades of plum and black make this top a little bit dark, a little bit dangerous. The front of this camisole is gently shaped for a more elegant fit.

pattern notes

For best fit, choose the size closest to your actual chest measurements.

SPECIAL STITCHES

EXSC (EXTENDED SINGLE CROCHET): insert hook into next stitch and pull up a loop, yo and pull through first loop, yo and pull through remaining 2 loops

DC3TOG (DC 3 TOGETHER): (yo, insert hook into next stitch and pull up a loop, yo and pull through 2 loops) 3 times; yo and pull through remaining 4 loops—2 sts decreased

DC4TOG (DC 4 TOGETHER): (yo, insert hook into next stitch and pull up a loop, yo and pull through 2 loops) 4 times; yo and pull through remaining 5 loops—3 sts decreased

FRENCH SQUARE

Make 6.

Ch 6, sl st to form a ring.

ROUND 1: Ch 4, (dc in center of ring, ch 1) 11 times, sl st into 3rd ch at beginning of round to join.

ROUND 2: Sl st in next ch, ch 2, dc3tog into same ch, ch 2, dc4tog in next ch-sp, ch 3, *tr in next dc, ch 3, (dc4tog in next ch-sp, ch 2) twice, dc4tog in next ch-sp, ch 3**. Repeat from * to ** twice more, tr in next dc, ch 3, dc4tog in next ch-sp, ch 2, sl st in top of dc3tog at beginning of round to join.

ROUND 3: Ch 1, *sc in top of center cluster, ch 5, sl st at base of these 5 ch, ch 2, skip (ch-2-sp, cluster), work 5 dc in next ch-3-sp, ch 1, tr in tr, ch 1, 5 dc in next ch-3-sp, ch 2, skip (cluster, ch-2-sp)**. Repeat from * to ** three more times, sl st in first sc of round. Fasten off.

Wet block to squares to lie flat.

ASSEMBLE PANELS

Sew 2 strips of 3 squares each by joining at the ch-3 picots at the corners and ch-5 picots at the center side edge.

RIGHT FRONT

SETUP ROW: With right side facing, sl st in top right corner of one panel. You'll work down one long edge. Ch 1, sc in ch-sp, *ch 3, sc in 3rd dc, ch 3, sc in ch-sp, ch 3, sc in 3rd dc, ch 3, sc in ch-sp, sc in ch-sp on next square**. Repeat from * to ** until one entire long edge has been worked, ending with sc in final ch-sp at end of strip—51 sts. Turn.

ROW 1: Ch 2, hdc in each sc and 3 hdc in each ch-sp across row. Turn.

ROW 2: Ch 2, work 2 hdc in first st, hdc in each st across row—1 st increased. Turn.

ROWS 3–10: Repeat rows 1-2.

ROW 11: Work 1 row even.

ROW 12: Ch 2, hdc2tog, hdc across—1 st decreased. Turn.

ROW 13: Work even.

Repeat rows 12–13 a total of 4 times.

Continue even until side measures 5½ (6, 6½, 7, 7½, 8, 8½, 9)" from edge of squares.

Fasten off.

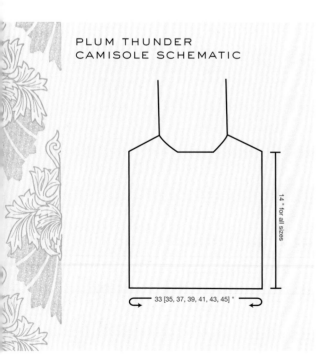

PLUM THUNDER
CAMISOLE SCHEMATIC

14" for all sizes

33 [35, 37, 39, 41, 43, 45] "

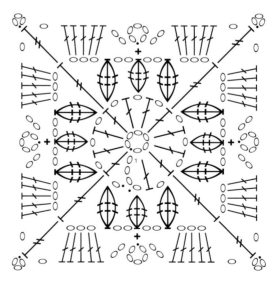

LEFT FRONT

With wrong side facing, and beginning at other corner of front panel, work as for Right Front.

BACK RIGHT

ROW 1: With second panel, work first two rows as for Right Front.

ROW 2: Ch 2, hdc in each hdc across.

Repeat row 2 until side measures same as front.

Fasten off.

BACK LEFT

ROWS 1–2: On opposite long edge of second panel, work first two rows as for Left Front.

ROW 3: Ch 2, hdc in each hdc across.

Repeat row 3 until side measures same as front.

Fasten off.

FINISHING

Sew in all ends.

Sew side seams.

SPAGHETTI STRAPS

Attach yarn with a sl st to top front point, ch 50, sl st to desired position on back. Repeat for other side.

Because the straps will stretch slightly when worn, you may wish to try on the top before determining the proper amount of ch sts for straps.

CHAPTER THREE

A TOUCH OF DRAMA

*skirts, dresses, and tops ideal for
a special night out (or in)*

sea pebble wrap
SKIRT

amy swenson

amy swenson

SIZES

XS (S, M, L, XL, 2X)

FINISHED MEASUREMENTS

WRAP WIDTH: 43 (48, 53, 58, 63, 68)"

LENGTH FROM WAIST TO HEM: 43 (48, 53, 58, 63, 68)"

YARN

YARN A: Alchemy Bamboo (100% bamboo; 138yds/50g): 7 (8, 9, 10, 11, 12) skeins, Mica (95M)

YARN B: Alchemy Bamboo (100% bamboo; 138yds/50g): 1 (1, 2, 2, 2, 2) skeins, Pewter (09M)

SUBSTITUTION: Approximately 942 (1072, 1193, 1378, 1516, 1654) yds DK-weight yarn in lighter color and 138 (138, 276, 276, 276, 276) yds DK-weight yarn in darker color. Look for yarn that knits to 22–24 sts/4".

HOOKS

US E/3.5mm crochet hook, or size needed to obtain proper gauge

NOTIONS

Yarn needle

2 1" buttons

Sewing needle and thread

GAUGE

After wet blocking, each square measures 2½" square.

Sturdy but sensual bamboo yarn in natural colors makes the perfect medium for this organically inspired skirt. Individual, pebblelike squares are crocheted, then crocheted together into strips. A perfect fit can be accomplished by sewing the button closures in place while wearing.

Because this bamboo yarn is dyed using only natural processes, some of the dye will shift when washed or rinsed. The effect you see in the photos, of almost denim dyeing, is created by gently rinsing the fabric in cold water. Like what you see? Adding a small amount of white vinegar to the rinse will help set the dye.

pattern notes

The provided width of the rectangle is when laid flat. Because you'll be wearing the rectangle as a wrap skirt, each size can fit an actual waist measurement of one-half to three-fifths of of the actual rectangle size. For example, the S size comfortably fits a waist of 24–28", and the M fits a waist sized from 26½–32".

The length of the skirt can be easily adjusted by adding additional rows of squares. Each additional row will add approximately 2½" in length.

SEA PEBBLE SQUARE

With Yarn B, make 18 (18, 24, 28, 30, 34) Sea Pebble Squares.

With Yarn A, make 115 (129, 137, 147, 159, 169) Sea Pebble Squares.

Wet block all squares until dry.

ROUND 1: Ch 3 (counts as 1 dc), work 11 dc into first ch, sl st to top of initial ch-3 to join.

ROUND 2: Ch 3 (counts as 1 dc), 2 dc in 1st dc, (dc in next 2 dc, 3 dc in next dc) 3 times, dc in next 2 dc, sl st to top of ch-3 to join.

ROUND 3: Ch 3 (counts as 1 dc), 2 dc in 1st dc, (dc in next 4 dc, 3 dc in next dc) 3 times, dc in next 4 dc, sl st to top of ch-3 to join.

ROUND 4: Ch 3 (counts as 1 dc), 2 dc in 1st dc, (dc in next 6 dc, 3 dc in next dc) 3 times, dc in next 6 dc, sl st to top of ch-3 to join.

Fasten off.

ASSEMBLY

Lay out squares in desired configuration, scattering the Yarn B squares more or less evenly throughout the set. Rectangle will be 7 squares tall and 19 (21, 23, 25, 27, 29) squares wide.

With Yarn A and wrong side of squares facing, sc in back loops of squares to join into horizontal strips 19 (21, 23, 25, 27, 29) strips wide and 2 squares tall. Add additional rows of squares in this way until you have a 7-strip-tall rectangle.

With right side facing, crochet strips together vertically to emphasize the vertical lines and complete the seaming.

FINISHING

ROUNDS 1–2: With Yarn A, work 2 rounds hdc evenly around outside edge of rectangle, working 3 hdc into each corner of the rectangle.

ROUND 3: With right side facing, work a button loop at the upper right corner as follows: hdc to corner stitch, ch 5, hdc in next st, continue around to next top corner, repeat button loop, finish hdc to end of round. Fasten off.

Sew in all ends.

At this point, it's extremely important to wet block skirt to get the squares to lay flat. To do this, submerge the piece in lukewarm water until thoroughly saturated. Gently squeeze out excess water. Lay flat on a towel in a well-ventilated area and stretch until the skirt is the desired measurements. If you have a spare mattress, rug, or blocking board, it's helpful to use rustproof pins to secure in place.

Allow to air dry.

Try on skirt and mark desired position for buttons. Sew buttons in place.

trellis boatneck
SHELL

amy swenson

SIZES

S (M, L, XL, 2X, 3X)

FINISHED MEASUREMENTS

CHEST: 34 (38, 42, 46, 50, 54)"

YARN

Jade Sapphire 6-ply Cashmere (100% cashmere; 150yds/55g): 3 (3, 4, 4, 5, 5) skeins, Hydrangea

SUBSTITUTION: Approximately 328 (383, 437, 492, 547, 601) yds aran-weight yarn. Look for yarn that knits to 18–20 sts/4".

HOOKS

US G7/4.5mm crochet hook, or size needed to obtain proper gauge

NOTIONS

Yarn needle

GAUGE

16 hdc equals 4"

A simple and modern trellis is the perfect stitch pattern for this body-hugging shell. Wear it as a vest or over a camisole. Dress it up or down, depending on your mood. Here, I used a pure cashmere hand-dyed yarn to combine the depth of color with the soft plushness of the fiber. But, it would be equally stunning in any luxury fiber. Try silk for a sparkly, evening-worthy look, or soft merino for work-ready fashion. This simple top can be worked up in a weekend.

pattern notes

Because this top is fitted in the waist and looser across the bust, look for 2–3" of ease for best fit.

WAISTBAND

Ch 26.

ROW 1: Hdc in 2nd ch from hook and every ch across. Turn.

ROW 2: Ch 2, hdc in each hdc across. (Do not work turning ch). Turn.

Repeat row 2 until band measures 28 (32, 36, 40, 44, 48)" from beginning. Do not cut yarn.

Sl st seam foundation chain to final row to form a tube.

BODICE

Worked in joined rounds without turning.

ROUND 1: Ch 1, sc 108 (120, 132, 144, 156, 168) evenly around top edge of band. Sl st to join.

ROUND 2: Ch 1, sc in 1st sc, (ch 3, skip 2 sc, sc in next sc) to last 2 sc, ch 3, sl st in initial sc; 36 (40, 44, 48, 52, 56) ch-sp.

TRELLIS PATTERN

ROUND 1: Ch 5, dc in next sc, (ch3, dc in next sc) around, ch 3, sl st to turning ch.

ROUND 2: Ch 1, sc in ch-sp made by previous row's turning ch, (ch 3, sc in next sc) around, ch 3, sl st to sc.

ROUND 3: Ch 6, tr in next sc, (ch 3, tr in next sc) around, ch 3, sl st to turning ch.

ROUND 4: Ch 1, sc in ch-sp made by previous row's turning ch, (ch 3, sc in next sc) around, ch 3, sl st to sc.

Repeat rounds 1–4 2 (2, 3, 3, 3) times more.

Fasten off.

Split for armholes and continue to work Back as follows.

BACK

Worked back and forth in rows.

ROW 1: Reattach yarn with a sl st to the 3rd sc of round.

Continuing in Trellis Pattern, work as for round 1 over the first 14 (16, 18, 20, 22, 24) ch-sp, ending with dc in sc. Turn.

Continue in Trellis Pattern (working back and forth as for rounds 1–4 above) over just these stitches until piece measures 8 (8½, 9, 9, 9½, 9½)" from beginning of underarm or to desired armhole height. Fasten off.

Reattach yarn with a sl st to the 4th sc from left edge of back. Work as for front.

FINISHING

Sew 2 (2, 2½, 3, 3½, 3½)" shoulder seams, or as desired.

Weave in any ends.

TRELLIS BOATNECK
SHELL SCHEMATIC

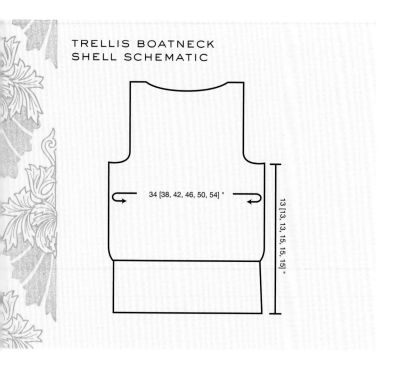

34 [38, 42, 46, 50, 54] "

13 [13, 13, 15, 15, 15] "

amy swenson

Sometimes the easiest shapes can be the most fun, and the most flattering. I've loved the recent "poof" trends in the fashion world. A few gathers here, a wide hem there—a little bit of poof gives any fabric more than a touch of fun. Here, a laceweight silk/mohair yarn is used to create an airy, semisheer skirt. This skirt is perfect for layering over a dramatic slip, or, for a more casual look, leggings.

SIZES

XS (S, M, L, XL, 2X, 3X)

FINISHED MEASUREMENTS

WAIST CIRCUMFERENCE: 28 (30, 32, 34, 36, 38, 40)"

YARN

Rowan Kidsilk Haze (70% kid mohair, 30% silk; 230yds/25g): 3 (3, 4, 4, 4, 4, 5) skeins, Dewberry (600)

SUBSTITUTION: Approximately 634 (678, 722, 765, 831, 897, 962) yds lace-weight mohair.

HOOKS

US E/3.5mm hook

US H/5.0mm hook, or size to obtain proper gauge

NOTIONS

Yarn needle

GAUGE

12 dc and 6½ rows of dc with size H/5.0mm hook

This fabric is very stretchy—when measuring your swatch give it a good shake to make sure it's not stretched, then lay it flat before measuring.

pattern notes

When in doubt, choose a smaller size than your actual waist measurements. The crocheted waistband is stretchy!

SIMPLE SHEER SKIRT SCHEMATIC

28 [30, 32, 34, 36, 38, 40] "

14 [14, 14, 15, 15, 16, 16, 17] "

WAISTBAND

With a double strand of yarn and US E/3.5mm hook, ch 6, turn. Dc in 3rd ch and each ch across. Turn.

Ch 3, dc in each dc.

Repeat last row until waistband measures 26 (28, 30, 32, 34, 36, 38, 40)" or as desired. Cut yarn, fasten off.

With yarn needle, sew short ends of band together.

SKIRT

Worked in joined rounds without turning.

ROUND 1: With a single strand of yarn and US H/5mm hook, attach with a sl st to edge of band. Ch 1, working around one side edge of the waistband sc around working approx. 4 sc for each dc row edge. Sl st to join.

ROUND 2: Ch 3, dc in each stitch around, sl st to join.

Repeat round 2 until skirt measures 14 (14, 14, 15, 15, 16, 16, 17)" from top edge of band, desired length.

Fasten off.

FINISHING

Weave in any ends.

japonais
TUNIC

amy swenson

Because crocheted tops are often layered over a cami or tank, why not design them with deeply plunging neck-lines? This Japanese-inspired long-sleeve tunic features a semisolid dc eyelet pattern along the cuffs and hem and a more open mesh pattern along the yoke and sleeves. It's crocheted like a cardigan and seamed up the front. Want a higher neckline? Just sew it up a little more.

pattern notes

This top is crocheted in one piece, in rows, from the bottom hem. The sleeves are then worked separately, then attached to the body so the yoke can be crocheted together.

SIZES

S (M, L, XL)

FINISHED MEASUREMENTS

CHEST: 36 (40, 44, 48)"

YARN

Lorna's Laces Lion and Lamb (50% merino wool, 50% silk; 205yds/100g): 6 (6, 7, 7) skeins, Red Rover

SUBSTITUTION: Approximately 1100 (1200, 1400, 1500) yds aran-weight yarn. Look for yarn that knits to 18 sts/4".

HOOKS

US G7/4.5mm hook, or size needed to obtain proper gauge

NOTIONS

Yarn needle

Removeable stitch markers

GAUGE

14 dc to 4"

EYELET PATTERN

Pattern is shown in rows but can be converted to rounds by simply joining the last st with a sl st to turning ch from the begining of the row.

Ch a multiple of 2 sts.

ROW 1: Ch 2, dc in each ch. Turn.

ROW 2: Ch 1, sc in each dc. Turn.

ROW 3: Ch 2, dc in each sc. Turn.

ROW 4: Ch 1, sc in each dc. Turn.

ROW 5: (Ch 3, sc in 2nd sc) to end. Turn.

ROW 6: Ch 1, 2 sc in each ch-3-sp. Turn.

ROW 7: Ch 2, dc in each sc. Turn.

ROWS 8–10: Repeat rows 4–6.

ROW 11: Ch 2, dc in each sc. Turn.

Repeat rows 2–11.

BODY

Ch 126 (140, 154, 168).

Work Eyelet Pattern rows 1–11, then rows 2–11 twice more, then rows 2–6.

DEEP NECK SHAPING

ROW 1: Ch 3, dc in 3rd sc, *(ch 1, dc in 2nd sc). Repeat from * to last 3 sc, ch 1, dc in last sc on row; (1 ch-sp decreased). Turn.

ROW 2: Ch 1, sc in 1st ch-sp, 2 sc in each following ch-sp to last ch-sp, 1 sc in ch-sp; (2 sc decreased).

Repeat last 2 rows 4 times more; 106 (120, 134, 148) sts remain.

Do not cut yarn, set body aside.

SLEEVES

Make 2. Worked in joined rounds without turning.

Ch 34 (38, 42, 46), sl st to join and begin working in rounds.

Work dc Eyelet Pattern rows 1–11, then rows 2–4.

On next round, begin sleeve increases as follows:

ROUND 1: Ch 4, *(dc in 2nd sc, ch 1). Repeat from * around, sl st to ch-4 to join.

ROUND 2: Ch 1, 2 sc in each ch-sp around, sl st to join.

ROUND 3: Ch 4, dc in 1st sc, ch 1, *(dc in 2nd sc, ch 1). Repeat from * around, sl st to join.

ROUND 4: Ch 1, 2 sc in each ch-sp around, sl st to join.

Repeat rounds 1–4 until you have 52 (56, 60, 64) sts—9 times.

Repeat rounds 1 and 2 until sleeve measures 18" or to desired length to underarm, end after working round 2. Place a marker on each sleeve at beginning of the round to mark the underarm.

Cut yarn and secure.

YOKE

You'll now be attaching the sleeves in 2 spots at the edge of each underarm, leaving a small gap of 8 sts under the arm to be sewn later.

Place markers for side seams of the sweater as follows: Mark the 22nd (24th, 28th, 32nd) sc in from each front edge.

Following the instructions for the Deep Neck Shaping, work row 1 then join the sleeves to the body as follows:

ROW 1: Work in pattern across front to 4 sc before side marker, end placing a dc ch 1 in 5th sc before marker.

Pick up 1st sleeve, join with dc in 5th sc before underarm marker. Continue in pattern, working through both sleeve and body sts, beginning with a ch 1, to 4 sts before sleeve underarm, end with dc ch 1 in 5th st before sleeve underarm marker.

Place next dc in 5th st after body side marker. Continue across back to 4 st before other side marker, ending with dc ch 1 in 5th st before marker instead of 6th (i.e., for last dc before sleeve, skip 2 st instead of 1).

Work across other sleeve and join to other front as before.

ROW 2: Ch 2, work 2 sc in each ch-sp across row. Turn.

JAPONAIS TUNIC SCHEMATIC

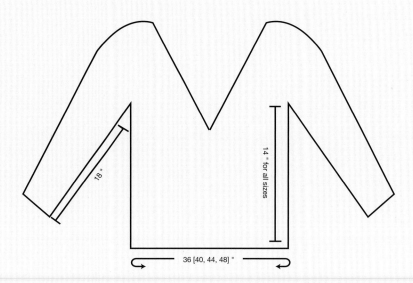

18"

14" for all sizes

36 [40, 44, 48] "

YOKE DECREASES

ROW 1: Ch 3, dc in 3rd sc, (ch 1, dc in 2nd sc) to end of row; 87 (98, 109, 120) ch-sp. Turn.

ROW 2: Ch 1, work 2 sc in first 4 ch-sp, 1 sc in next ch-sp, (2 sc in next 5 ch-sp, 1 sc in next ch-sp) to last 4 ch-sp, 2 sc in last 4 ch-sp. Turn.

ROW 3 AND ALL ODD ROWS: Repeat row 1.

ROW 4: Ch 1, work 2 sc in each ch-sp to end of row. Turn.

ROW 6: Ch 1, work 2 sc in first 6 ch-sp, 1 sc in next ch-sp, (2 sc in next 5 ch-sp, 1 sc in next ch-sp) to last 6 ch-sp, 2 sc in last 6 ch-sp. Turn.

ROW 8: Ch 1, work 2 sc in each ch-sp to end of row. Turn.

ROW 10: Ch 1, work 2 sc in first 2 ch-sp, 1 sc in next ch-sp, (2 sc in next 4 ch-sp, 1 sc in next ch-sp) to last 2 ch-sp, 2 sc in last 2 ch-sp. Turn.

ROW 12: Ch 1, work 2 sc in each ch-sp to end of row. Turn.

ROW 14: Ch 1, 2 sc in first 5 ch-sp, 1 sc in next ch-sp, (2 sc in next 4 ch-sp, 1 sc in next ch-sp) to last 5 ch-sp, 2 sc in last 5 ch-sp. Turn.

ROW 16: Ch 1, work 2 sc in each ch-sp to end of row. Turn.

ROW 18: Ch 1, work 2 sc in first 2 ch-sp, 1 sc in next ch-sp, (2 sc in next 3 ch-sp, 1 sc in next ch-sp) to last 3 ch-sp, work 2 sc in each of last 3 ch-sp. Turn.

ROW 19: Ch 3, dc in 3rd sc, (ch 1, dc in 2nd sc) to end of row; 47 (58, 69, 80) ch-sp. Turn.

FOR SIZE M ONLY

ROW 20: Ch 1, work 2 sc in each ch-sp to end of row. Turn.

ROW 22: Turn. Ch 1, 2 sc in first 5 ch-sp, 1 sc in next ch-sp, (2 sc in next 4 ch-sp, 1 sc in next ch-sp) to last 6 ch-sp, 2 sc in 5 ch-sp, 1 sc in next ch-sp. Turn.

ROW 24: Turn. Ch 1, work 2 sc in each ch-sp to end of row. Turn.

ROW 25: Turn. Ch 3, dc in 3rd sc, (ch 1, 2 dc in second sc) to end of row—51 ch-sp. Turn.

FOR SIZE L ONLY

ROW 20: Ch 1, work 2 sc in each ch-sp to end of row. Turn.

ROW 22: Ch 1, 2 sc in first 3 ch-sp, 1 sc in next ch-sp, (2 sc in next 4 ch-sp, 1 sc in next ch-sp) to last 4 ch-sp, 2 sc in 4 ch-sp. Turn.

ROW 24: Ch 1, work 2 sc in each ch-sp to end of row. Turn.

ROW 26: Ch 1, 2 sc in first 3 ch-sp, 1 sc in next ch-sp, (2 sc in next 3 ch-sp, 1 sc in next ch-sp) to last 4 ch-sp, 2 sc in 4 ch-sp. Turn.

ROW 28: Ch 1, work 2 sc in each ch-sp to end of row. Turn.

ROW 29: Ch 3, dc in 3rd sc, (ch 1, dc in 2nd sc) to end of row—52 ch-sp. Turn.

FOR SIZE XL ONLY

ROW 20: Ch 1, work 2 sc in each ch-sp to end of row. Turn.

ROW 22: Ch 1, 2 sc in first 4 ch-sp, 1 sc in next ch-sp, (2 sc in next 4 ch-sp, 1 sc in next ch-sp) to last 4 ch-sp, 2 sc in 4 ch-sp. Turn.

ROW 24: Ch 1, work 2 sc in each ch-sp to end of row. Turn.

ROW 26: Ch 1, 2 sc in first 4 ch-sp, 1 sc in next ch-sp, (2 sc in next 3 ch-sp, 1 sc in next ch-sp) to last 4 ch-sp, 2 sc in 4 ch-sp. Turn.

ROW 28: Ch 1, work 2 sc in each ch-sp to end of row. Turn.

ROW 30: Ch 1, 2 sc in first 3 ch-sp, 1 sc in next ch-sp, (2 sc in next 3 ch-sp, 1 sc in next ch-sp) to last 4 ch-sp, 2 sc in 4 ch-sp. Turn.

ROW 32: Ch 1, work 2 sc in each ch-sp to end of row. Turn.

ROW 33: Ch 3, dc in 3rd sc, (ch1, dc in 2nd sc) to end of row—52 ch-sp. Turn.

FOR ALL SIZES

Fasten off.

FINISHING

FRONT FACING

ROW 1: With right side facing, attach yarn with sl st to bottom right front corner. Ch 1, sc evenly along front edge to beginning of mesh section, then work 2 sc in each dc and 1 sc in each sc along mesh section of front. Work 2 sc into each ch-sp across neckline, then 2 sc in each dc and 1 sc in each sc of left mesh edge, then sc evenly along left bottom edge. Turn.

ROW 2: Ch 3, dc in each sc, working 2 dc in each top corner where front meets the neckline.

SEW UP FRONT

Fasten off, leaving a 2-foot tail. Use tail to sew fronts together to beginning of V-neck shaping.

Weave in any ends.

Wet block.

wave cocktail
DRESS

annie modesitt

SIZES

XS (S, M, L, XL, 2X)

FINISHED MEASUREMENTS

BUST: 32 (36, 40, 44, 48, 52)"

FINISHED LENGTH FROM SHOULDER: 43¾
(47½, 49¼, 52¼, 55¼, 53)"

YARN

YARN A: Karabella Zodiac (100% cotton;
98yds/50g): 8 (9, 9, 10, 10, 11) skeins, Spring
Green (422)

YARN B: Karabella Vintage Cotton (100% cotton;
140yds/50g): 7 (8, 8, 9, 9, 10) skeins, Teal Blue
(300)

SUBSTITUTION: Look for DK-weight cottons in
two colors. A total of 1750–2515 yds of yarn is
required.

HOOKS

US G/4.0mm hook

US H/5.0mm hook

US I/5.5mm hook

NOTIONS

Yarn needle

GAUGE

20 sts and 8 rows = 4" wide by 5" tall in wave
pattern and size US G/4.0mm hook

Inspired by delightful (and sometimes oh-so-cutesy)
cocktail dresses of the late '50s, this dress can be worn
with a wink and a smile. Its summery color palette uses
shades of blue, yellow, and green to call to mind beach-
side patios and fresh mojitos. A simple wave pattern
lends the fabric a retro texture, while the clever mesh top
design lets you be daring and demure at the same time.

pattern notes

For best fit, select a size 1–2" larger than your actual bust measurement.

*Annie Modesitt enjoys the sculptural nature of crochet and the fact that
beautiful fabric can be made using just a hook and a string—like catching a fish! Annie's designs and essays about knitting and crochet can be
found in several books and magazines, including* Interweave Crochet,
Family Circle, *and* Easy Knitting. *Annie is the editor of the 2006 and
2007 Accord* Crochet Pattern-a-Day *calendars.*

SPECIAL STITCH

TR2TOG (DECREASE): yo twice, insert hook into next st, yo, pull up a loop, yo insert hook into next st, yo, pull up a lp, work sts off hook two at a time as for a standard treble

DECORATIVE CHAIN EMBROIDERY

Holding the yarn at the back of the work, insert the hook from the front to the back. Yo, draw loop through to the front of the fabric. (Move hook to point where next chain should start and insert from the front to the back. Yo, draw loop through fabric and through loop on hook.) Repeat, moving the hook at the start of each new stitch to create a decorative pattern on the front of the fabric.

TWISTED CORD

Measure a length of yarn 4 times longer than desired length of final twisted cord. Fold the strand in half and make a slipknot at the cut ends. Pass the slipknot over a doorknob and stand far enough away so that the yarn hangs in midair and does not touch the ground.

Slip a crochet hook into the slipknot you are holding in your hand and pull the cord taut so that the hook rests perpendicular to your fingers allowing the yarn to slip between your middle and pointer finger.

Begin turning the hook—similar to the way that the propeller on a toy plane twists a rubber band—to twist the strands of yarn. Continue twisting until the yarn is quite taut and evenly twisted. When relaxed slightly the twisted yarn should want to kink up.

Still holding one end of the yarn in your left hand, with your right hand pinch the twisted strand midway between yourself and the doorknob.

Bring the ends of the yarn together by moving toward the doorknob, but DO NOT LET GO OF THE MIDDLE OF THE TWISTED YARN. When the 2 slipknots are together you can release the middle of the cord, you will notice the yarn will twist around itself forming a plied cord.

Still holding tight to the slipknot ends, loose the yarn end from the doorknob and tie both ends together. You can run your finger between the cords to even out the twists if necessary.

WAVE STITCH PATTERN

Worked over a multiple of 7 sts.

BEGIN 4-ROW WAVE PATTERN

Worked in rounds without turning.

ROUND 1: With Yarn A, ch 1, (sc, hdc in next 2 sts, dc in next 2 sts, tr in next 2 sts, dc in next 2 sts, hdc in next 2 sts, sc in next 2 sts), repeat to end, join with a sl st.

ROUND 2: Ch 1, sc around.

ROUND 3: With Yarn B, ch 3, (tr, dc in next 2 sts, hdc in next 2 sts, sc in next 3 sts, hdc in next 2 sts, dc in next 2 sts, tr in next 2 sts), repeat to end, join with a sl st.

ROUND 4: Repeat round 2.

SKIRT

Work joined in the round from the bottom up without turning.

With G/4.0mm hook and Yarn A, ch 154 (182, 196, 224, 238, 266) sts, join to work in the round.

SETUP ROUND: Sc around.

Repeat rounds (see chart), stranding color not currently used up along wrong side of work. Continue repeating rounds 1–4 until piece measures 11¼ (11½, 11¾, 12, 12¼, 12½)" from foundation chain, end with row 4 of pattern chart.

SKIRT DECREASES

Continue changing yarns every 2 rows as established.

In next repeat, dec as follows:

ROUND 1: (Sc, hdc in next 2 sts, dc in next 2 sts, tr, tr2tog, hdc in next 2 sts, hdc in next 2 sts, sc in next 2 sts), repeat to end of round—143 (169, 182, 208, 221, 247).

ROUNDS 2 AND 4: Sc around

ROUND 3: (Tr, dc in next 2 sts, hdc in next 2 sts, sc in next 2 sts, hdc in next 2 sts, dc in next 2 sts, tr2tog), repeat to end of round—132 (158, 171, 197, 210, 236).

Work even in pattern as established for 8 (8, 12, 12, 16, 16) rounds, then dec as follows:

ROUND 1: (Sc, hdc in next 2 sts, dc in next 2 sts, tr2tog), repeat to end of round—121 (147, 160, 186, 199, 225).

ROUNDS 2 AND 4: Sc around.

ROUND 3: Skip 1 tr, (dc in next 2 sts, hdc in next 2 sts, sc, hdc in next 2 sts, dc in next 2 sts, tr2 tog), repeat to last Repeat, work final tr2tog with skip st from start of round—110 (136, 149, 175, 188, 214) sts.

Work even with no further decreasing until piece measures 22 (24, 26, 28, 30, 32)" from foundation chain.

UNDERBUST

Worked in Yarn A only.

ROUND 1: (1 hdc in each next 4 sts, skip 1, ch 1), repeat to end of round.

ROUNDS 2–4: 1 sc in each st or ch-sp.

Repeat rounds 1–4 1 (1, 2, 2, 3, 3) more times—8 (8, 12, 12, 16, 16) rounds total.

BUST

Worked in Yarn B only, and worked in spiraled rounds without turning.

Block work so far and determine which side will be the front.

ROUND 1: With G/4.0mm hook and front of dress facing you, join Yarn B at right side and sc 56 (68, 74, 88, 94, 108) across back.

Switch to size H/5.0mm hook (I/5.5mm hook for sizes L, XL, 2X), hdc 54 (68, 75, 87, 94, 106) across front to start of round.

Repeat round 1 16 (16, 16, 17, 17, 18) times, changing hook when moving from front to back, until piece measures 9¾ (10, 10¼, 10½, 10¾, 11)" from start of bust area (for a fuller bust, add a few more rounds).

Work 4 more rounds as above.

BUST EDGING

ROUNDS 1–4: Work as established with G/4.0mm hook across back, continue with G/4.0mm hook work hdc across front as in prev rounds.

BUST DECORATIVE CHAIN CROCHET

ROW 1: With G/4.0mm hook and Yarn B and starting at first hdc at lower right front, work decorative chain embroidery across entire row to last hdc at lower left front. Chain up to first hdc in next row.

ROW 2: Repeat last row in opposite direction across front to last hdc in second row from underbust at lower right front. Chain up to first hdc in next row.

Repeat row 2 until all front bust rows have been covered with Decorative Chain Embroidery. Fasten off and weave in ends.

BACK LACE YOKE

Worked in Yarn A only.

Count 11 (8, 9, 13, 9, 13) sts from the right under-arm edge at point where crochet hook size changed from H/5.0mm to G/4.0mm.

With G/4.0mm hook join a strand of Yarn A to next st.

ROW 1 (RS): (Ch 7, skip 4, sc in next st) 9 (12, 13, 15, 17, 19) times, turn.

ROW 2 (WS): Ch 7, sc into first ch-sp, (ch 7, sc into next ch-sp), repeat to last ch-sp. End ch 7, sl st into point where Yarn A was joined, turn.

ROW 3 (RS): 1 sl st into each last 3 chains worked, sc into ch-sp, (ch 7, sc into next ch-sp), repeat to last ch-sp, turn.

ROW 4 (WS): Ch 7, sc into first ch-sp, (ch 7, sc into next ch-sp), repeat to last ch-sp. End ch 7, sl st into first sc from prev row. Turn.

NOTE: On wrong side rows there will be one more ch-sp than in right side rows.

Repeat last 2 rows until piece measures 3¾ (4, 4¼, 4½, 4¾, 5)", or reaches to just below nape of neck. End with a wrong side row.

DIVIDE FOR NECK

ROW 1 (RS): 1 sl st into each last 3 chains worked, sc into ch-sp, (ch 7, sc into next ch-sp) 3 (4, 5, 5, 5, 7) times. Turn.

ROW 2 (WS): Ch 7, sc into first ch-sp, (ch 7, sc into next ch-sp), repeat to last ch-sp. End ch 7, sl st into first sc from prev row, turn work.

Repeat rows 1–2, creating a shoulder strap that will travel over the shoulder to the front. Work until strap measures 4¼ (4½, 4¾, 5, 5¼, 5½)" from neck divide.

ATTACHING STRAPS

Working with opposite side of Back Lace Yoke, repeat front strap shaping for other shoulder.

Try dress on to determine placement of front straps along top edge of front of dress bodice.

With a needle and thread tack the front shoulder strap to the top front edge, spacing tacks every 5 sts to match placement of yoke lace at top of back.

LACE HEM

With G/4.0mm hook join a strand of B to center back of skirt bottom.

(Ch 7, skip 4, sc in next st), repeat around entire hem, end 1 sc in first ch-sp formed.

(Ch 7, sc in next ch-sp), repeat, working in a spiral, until lace hem measures 2" or desired length. End with sc at center back, tie off.

WAVE COCKTAIL DRESS SCHEMATIC

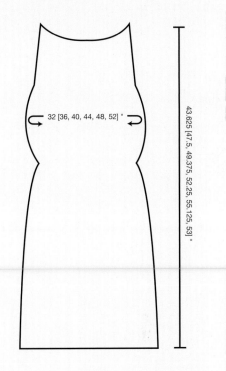

32 [36, 40, 44, 48, 52] "

43.625 [47.5, 49.375, 52.25, 55.125, 53] "

FINISHING

Block dress. Weave in ends.

MAKE CORDS

Create 3 twisted cords whose finished length is twice the waist measurement, following Twisted Cord instruction. Starting at right side of body, weave each cord through chain spaces in one of the 3 eyelet rows in underbust section. Cords will be loosened when dress is put on and tightened when it's on to create a firm underbust area which will act like a mini-corset and will support the bust area.

seaside romance
SKIRT

amie hirtes

SIZES

XS (S, M, L, XL, 2X)

FINISHED MEASUREMENTS

LOW WAIST: 31 (33, 35, 37, 39, 41)"

YARN

YARN A: South West Trading Company Oasis (100% soy silk; 240yds/100g): 6 (6, 7, 7, 8, 8) skeins, Turquoise (502)

YARN B: South West Trading Company Shimmer (50% nylon, 50% polyester; 150yds/25g): 2 (4, 4, 4, 6, 6) skeins, Copper (405)

SUBSTITUTION: Look for light DK- or sport-weight yarns that knit to 22–24 sts/4".

HOOKS

US C/2.75mm

US D/3.25mm

NOTIONS

Yarn needle

3 ⅝" (16mm) buttons

1 10" invisible zipper to match Yarn A

Sewing needle and thread to match Yarn A

Removeable stitch markers

GAUGE

22 sc to 4" on D/3.25mm hook

Created from the most sumptuous soy silk yarn, this low-waisted A-line skirt is sure to flatter most silhouettes and is offered in a range of sizes. A decorative gold and turquoise waistband delivers a well-defined midsection while three tiers of fabric float away from the body. Shell and picot stitches combine to form the lacey bottom tier. A feminine, gold-accented edging is worked around each tier. Buttons and an invisible zipper add to the tailored look. Pair it with gold sandals and an airy top for a romantic summer evening.

pattern notes

Skirt is meant to hang low on the waist. Select a size a few inches larger than your actual waist measurements, or measure at the hip bone.

Where pattern calls for Yarn B, work two strands together.

Amie Hirtes grew up at the Jersey Shore in a busy tourist town. The Jersey Shore color palette—warm blues and cool grays, muted pastels, and washed out browns—continues to be the source of inspiration for Amie. Additionally, some of the garments she produces for her online site, NexStitch (www.nexstitch.com), reflect her continuing interest in a simple, beachlike aesthetic. Not so coincidentally, her all-time favorite stitch continues to be the shell stitch due to its versatility.

SPECIAL STITCHES

BPHDC (BACK POST HALF DOUBLE CROCHET): yo, insert hook around stem (post) of next stitch from back to front to back, yo, pull up a loop, yo and draw through remaining loops

BPDC (BACK POST DOUBLE CROCHET): yo, insert hook around stem (post) of next stitch from back to front to back, yo, pull up a loop, yo, draw through two loops, yo and draw through remaining loops

BPTR (BACK POST TREBLE CROCHET): yo two times, insert hook around stem (post) of next stitch from back to front to back, yo, pull up a loop, (yo, draw though two loops) three times

DC2TOG (DOUBLE CROCHET 2 TOGETHER): (yo, insert hook in next stitch, yo, pull up a loop, yo, draw through two loops) twice, yo, and draw through all loops on hook

SC3TOG (SINGLE CROCHET 3 TOGETHER): (insert hook in next stitch, yo, pull up a loop) three times, yo, and draw through all loops on hook

SM SHELL (SMALL SHELL): [(dc, ch 1) twice, dc] in stitch indicated

MED SHELL (MEDIUM SHELL): [(dc, ch 2) twice, dc] in stitch indicated

LG SHELL (LARGE SHELL): [(dc, ch 3) twice, dc] in stitch indicated

PS (PICOT STITCH): (sc, ch 3, sc) in stitch indicated

WAISTBAND

Skirt is worked top-down from the waist.

FOUNDATION: With Yarn A and larger hook, ch 142 (154, 166, 178, 190, 202).

ROUND 1 (RS): Working in blo, sc in 2nd ch and each ch across to last ch, 5 sc in last ch. Working back along base ch in unused loops, sc across to last ch, 4 sc in last ch, join with sl st to 1st sc and switch to Yarn B, do not turn; 288 (312, 336, 360, 384, 408) sc made.

ROUND 2: Ch 2 (counts as 1st hdc now and throughout), hdc in same st as sl st, sl st in next sc, *2 hdc, sl st* Repeat 69 (75, 81, 87, 93, 99) more times, **2 hdc in same sc as last sl st, (sl st, 2 hdc, sl st) in next sc, (2 hdc, sl st) in next sc**. Repeat * to * 71 (77, 83, 89, 95, 101) times. Repeat ** to ** once, join with sl st to 1st sc and switch to Yarn A, do not turn—296 (320, 344, 368, 392, 416) hdc made.

ROUND 3: Ch 2, bphdc in next hdc, skip sl st, *bphdc in next 2 hdc, skip sl st*. Repeat 69 (75, 81, 87, 93, 99) more times, **2 BPhdc in next 2 hdc, skip sl st**, repeat * to * once, repeat ** to ** once, repeat * to * 71 (77, 83, 89, 95, 101) times, repeat ** to ** once, repeat * to * once, repeat ** to ** once, join with sl st to 1st hdc and switch to Yarn B, do not turn; 304 (328, 352, 376, 400, 424) bphdc made.

SEASIDE ROMANCE SKIRT SCHEMATIC

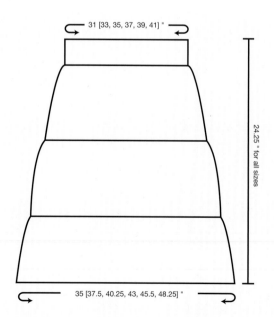

31 [33, 35, 37, 39, 41] "

24.25 " for all sizes

35 [37.5, 40.25, 43, 45.5, 48.25] "

more times, **(bpdc, bptr) in next hdc, ch 1, (bpdc, bptr) in next hdc, skip sl st**, repeat * to * 5 times, repeat ** to ** once, repeat * to * 75 (81, 87, 93, 99, 105) times, repeat ** to ** once, (bphdc, ch 8, sl st in back thread of 1st ch (button loop made), bphdc, skip sl st, 2 bphdc, skip sl st) 2 more times, omitting last 2 hdc but skping next sl st, repeat ** to ** once (place marker on second to last ch 1), sl st to 1st hdc. Finish off—336 (360, 384, 408, 432, 456) BP sts and 3 button loops made.

BODY TIER 1

Worked back and forth in rows.

ROW 1: Remove marker. With larger hook and Yarn A, sl st to back thread of ch 1, hdc in same st, 4 bphdc, inc, *5 bphdc, inc*, repeat * to * across to next corner, placing last inc in back thread of ch 1, turn—182 (196, 210, 224, 238, 252) sts made made.

ROWS 2–10: Ch 2, hdc in 2nd st and in each st across, turn—182 (196, 210, 224, 238, 252) hdc made.

ROW 11: Ch 2, hdc in 2nd st and in next 4 sts, inc, *6 hdc, inc* across, turn—208 (224, 240, 256, 272, 288) hdc made.

ROWS 12–26: Ch 2, hdc in 2nd st and in each st across, turn—208 (224, 240, 256, 272, 288) hdc made.

BODY TIER 2

Worked back and forth in rows.

ROW 1: Ch 2 (place stitch marker #2), working in bk loops, hdc in 2nd st and in next 5 sts, inc, *7 hdc, inc* across, turn—234 (252, 270, 288, 306, 324) hdc made.

ROWS 2–12: Ch 2, hdc in 2nd st and in each st across, turn—234 (252, 270, 288, 306, 324) hdc made.

ROW 13: Ch 2, hdc in 2nd st and in next 6 sts, inc, *8 hdc, inc* across, turn—260 (280, 300, 320, 340, 360) hdc made.

ROWS 14–26: Ch 2, hdc in 2nd st and in each st across, join with sl st to 1st hdc, turn—260 (280, 300, 320, 340, 360) hdc made.

BODY TIER 3

Worked in the round.

ROUND 1: Ch 2 (place stitch marker #3), working in bk loops, hdc in 2nd st and in next 17 sts, inc, *19 hdc, inc* across, join with sl st to 1st st—273 (294, 315, 336, 357, 378) hdc made.

ROUND 2: Ch 1, sc in same st, ch 3, sc, skip 2 sts, sm shell, skip 2 sts, *sc, ch 3, sc, skip 2 sts, sm shell, skip 2 sts*, repeat * to * around, join with sl st to 1st sc—39 (42, 45, 48, 51, 54) sm shells made.

ROUND 4: Ch 2, hdc in same st as sl st, sl st in next bphdc, *2 hdc, sl st* Repeat 69 (75, 81, 87, 93, 99) more times, **((2 hdc, sl st) in next bphdc, 2 hdc, sl st) 3 times, (2 hdc, sl st) in next bphdc**, repeat * to *71 (77, 83, 89, 95, 101) times, repeat ** to ** once, join with sl st to 1st bphdc and switch to Yarn A, do not turn; 312 (336, 360, 384, 408, 432) hdc made.

ROUND 5: Ch 2, bphdc in next hdc, skip sl st, *2 bphdc, skip sl st*. Repeat 71 (77, 83, 89, 95, 101) more times, **2 bphdc in next hdc, ch 1, 2 bphdc in next hdc, skip sl st**, repeat * to * 3 times, repeat ** to ** once, repeat * to * 73 (79, 85, 91, 97, 103) times, repeat ** to ** once, repeat * to * 3 times, repeat ** to ** once, join with sl st to 1st hdc and switch to Yarn B, do not turn—320 (344, 368, 392, 416, 440) bphdc made.

ROUND 6: Ch 2, hdc in same st as sl st, sl st in next bphdc, *2 hdc, sl st*. Repeat 72 (78, 84, 90, 96, 102) more times, **(2 hdc, sl st) in ch-1-sp**, repeat * to * 5 times, repeat ** to ** once, repeat * to * 75 (81, 87, 93, 99, 105) times, repeat ** to ** once, repeat * to * 5 times, repeat ** to ** once, repeat * to * once, join with sl st to 1st bphdc and switch to Yarn A, do not turn—328 (352, 376, 400, 424, 448) hdc made.

ROUND 7: Ch 2, bphdc in next hdc, skip sl st, *2 bphdc, skip sl st*. Repeat 73 (79, 85, 91, 97, 103)

ROUND 3: Sl st in ps, ch 6 (counts as 1st dc and ch 3 now and throughout), ps in center dc of sm shell, ch 3, *dc in ps, ch 3, ps in center dc of sm shell, ch 3*, repeat from * to * around, join with sl st to 1st dc—40 (43, 46, 49, 52, 55) dc made.

ROUND 4: Ch 1, ps in same st, sm shell in next ps, *ps in dc, sm shell in next ps*, repeat * to * around, join with sl st to 1st sc; 39 (42, 45, 48, 51, 54) sm shells made.

ROUND 5: Repeat round 3.

ROUND 6: Repeat round 4.

ROUND 7: Repeat round 3.

ROUND 8: Ch 1, ps in same st, ch 1, med shell in next ps, ch 1 *ps in dc, ch 1, med shell in next ps*, repeat * to * around, join with sl st to 1st sc—39 (42, 45, 48, 51, 54) med shells made.

ROUND 9: Sl st in ps, ch 7 (counts as 1st dc and ch 4 now and throughout), ps in center dc of med shell, ch 4, *dc in ps, ch 4, ps in center dc of med shell, ch 4*, repeat from * to * around, join with sl st to 1st dc—40 (43, 46, 49, 52, 55) dc made.

ROUND 10: Repeat round 8.

ROUND 11: Repeat round 9.

ROUND 12: Repeat round 8.

ROUND 13: Repeat round 9.

Round 14: Ch 1, ps in same st, ch 2, lg shell in next ps, ch 2 *ps in dc, ch 2, lg shell in next ps, ch 2*, repeat * to * around, join with sl st to 1st sc—39 (42, 45, 48, 51, 54) lg shells made.

ROUND 15: Sl st in ps, ch 8 (counts as 1st dc and ch 5 now and throughout), ps in center dc of lg shell, ch 5, *dc in ps, ch 5, ps in center dc of lg shell, ch 5*, repeat from * to * around, join with sl st to 1st dc—40 (43, 46, 49, 52, 55) dc made.

ROUND 16: Repeat round 14.

ROUND 17: Repeat round 15.

ROUND 18: Repeat round 14.

ROUND 19: Sl st in ps, ch 8, sc in center dc of lg shell, ch 5, *dc in ps, ch 5, sc in center dc of lg shell, ch 5*, repeat from * to * around, join with sl st to 1st dc, do not finish off—40 (43, 46, 49, 52, 55) dc made.

TIER 3 EDGING

ROUND 1: Ch 3 (counts as 1st dc now and through-out), 4 dc in same st, sc in next ch-5-sp, ch 4, sc in next ch-5-sp, *5 dc in next dc, sc in next ch-5-sp, ch 4, sc in next ch-5-sp*, repeat * to * around, join with sl st to 1st dc and switch to Yarn B—195 (210, 225, 240, 255, 270) dc made.

ROUND 2: Ch 4 (counts as 1st dc and ch 1 now and throughout), working in bk loops, (dc in next dc, ch 1) four times, sc in ch-4-sp, ch 1, *(dc in next dc, ch 1) five times, sc in ch-4-sp, ch 1*. Repeat * to * around, join with sl st to 1st dc and switch to Yarn A—195 (210, 225, 240, 255, 270) dc made.

ROUND 3: Ch 5 (counts as 1st dc and ch 2 now and throughout), (dc in next dc, ch 2) three times, dc in next dc, ch 1, *(dc in next dc, ch 2) four times, dc in next dc, ch 1*. Repeat * to * around, join with sl st to 1st dc and switch to Yarn B and smaller hook—195 (210, 225, 240, 255, 270) dc made.

ROUND 4: With smaller hook and using Yarn B, sl st to 1st ch-2-sp from Row 3. Working in each ch-1 and ch-2-sp, ps across. Finish off—195 (210, 225, 240, 255, 270) ps made.

NOTE: Zipper Edging needs to be completed in order to work Tier 1 Edging directions.

ZIPPER EDGING

Remove marker #1. With right side facing, skirt on its side, and working from right to left, sl st to marked st using Yarn A. Working in bk posts of sts from waistband, hdc across to to next corner of waistband, sc down and up zipper hole, placing sc3tog at bottom corner by picking up sts in right, bottom, and left sides.

TIER 1 EDGING

ROW 1: Remove marker #2. With right side facing and skirt upside down, sl st to marked st using Yarn A. Working in free loops, ch 3, 2 dc in same st, skip 2 sts, sc, ch 1, skip 1 st, sc, skip 2 sts, *5 dc in next st, skip 2 sts, sc, ch 1, skip 1 st, sc, skip 2 sts*, repeat * to * around to last 2 sts, work last (3 dc) in same st by picking up loop from post on sc of zipper edging. Finish off—131 (141, 151, 161, 171, 181) dc made.

ROW 2: Using Yarn B, sl st to bk loop of 1st dc from Row 1. Ch 4, working in bk loops, dc in next dc, ch 1, dc in next dc, sc in ch-1-sp, *(dc in next dc, ch 1) four times, dc in next dc, sc in ch-1-sp*, repeat * to * around to last 3 dc, (dc, ch 1) twice, dc in last dc. Finish off—131 (141, 151, 161, 171, 181) dc made.

ROW 3: Using Yarn A, sl st to 1st dc from Row 2. Ch 5, dc in next dc, ch 2, dc2tog while skping next sc, *(ch 2, dc in next dc) three times, ch 2, dc2tog while skping next sc*, repeat * to * around to last 2 dc, dc in next dc, ch 2, dc in last dc. Finish off—131 (141, 151, 161, 171, 181) dc made.

ROW 4: With smaller hook and using Yarn B, sl st to 1st ch-2-sp from Row 3. Working in each ch-2-sp and free sp under dc2tog, ps across. Finish off—130 (140, 150, 160, 170, 180) ps made.

TIER 2 EDGING

ROUND 1: Remove marker #3. With right side facing and skirt upside down, sl st to marked st using Yarn A. Working in free loops, ch 3, 4 dc in same st, skip 2 sts, sc, ch 3, skip 3 sts, sc, skip 2 sts, *5 dc in next st, skip 2 sts, sc, ch 3, skip 3 sts, sc, skip 2 sts*, repeat * to * around, join with sl st to 1st dc and switch to Yarn B—130 (140, 150, 160, 170, 180) dc made.

ROUND 2: Ch 4, working in bk loops, (dc in next dc, ch 1) four times, sc in ch-3-sp, ch 1, *(dc in next dc, ch 1) five times, sc in ch-3-sp, ch 1*, repeat * to * around, join with sl st to 1st dc and switch to Yarn A—130 (140, 150, 160, 170, 180) dc made.

ROUND 3: Ch 5, (dc in next dc, ch 2) three times, dc in next dc, skip (ch 1, sc, ch 1), *(dc in next dc, ch 2) four times, dc in next dc, (ch 1, sc, ch 1)*, repeat * to * around, join with sl st to 1st dc and switch to Yarn B and smaller hook—130 (140, 150, 160, 170, 180) dc made.

ROUND 4: With smaller hook and using Yarn B, sl st to 1st ch-2-sp from Row 3. Working in each ch-2-sp and free sp where last and first dc of each lg shell meets, ps around, join with sl st to 1st sc. Finish off—130 (140, 150, 160, 170, 180) ps made.

FINISHING

With yarn needle, weave ends through stitches securely. Sew in zipper, aligning the top stops where the waistband meets Tier 1. Zipper pull tab should sit snuggly where zipper edging changes from hdc to sc sts. Sew buttons onto opposite side of waistband, so both ends of the waistband meet, but do not overlap.

forest path
SKIRT

amy swenson

This modern, romantic skirt was designed by updating a Victorian-inspired rose motif with tweedy alpaca yarn in a short-short length. Each square is crocheted individually, then attached by crocheting together with a decorative mesh. Finish it off with a shaped waistband and you're ready to frolic through the forest! Wear this one over a slinky silky slip, kicky leggings, or dare to go bare.

SIZES

S (M, L, XL)

FINISHED MEASUREMENTS

HIP: 36 (40, 44, 48)"

LENGTH FROM WAIST TO HEM: 15", for all sizes

YARN

YARN A: Rowan Felted Tweed (50% merino wool, 25% alpaca, 25% viscose; 191yds/50g): 3 (3, 4, 4) skeins, Bilberry (151)

YARN B: Rowan Felted Tweed (50% merino wool, 25% alpaca, 25% viscose; 191yds/50g): 1 (1, 2, 2) skeins, Sigh (148)

SUBSTITUTION: Approximately 383–547 yds DK-weight yarn in dark color and 109–273 yds DK-weight yarn in light color. Look for yarn that knits to 22–24 sts/4".

HOOKS

US D/3.25mm crochet hook, or size needed to obtain proper gauge

NOTIONS

Yarn needle

GAUGE

Each motif is 4" square, after blocking

pattern notes

The length of the skirt can be easily adjusted by adding additional rows of squares. Each additional row will add approximately 4" in length.

ROSE MOTIF

Worked in rounds without joining.

With Yarn B, ch 8, join with sl st to form ring.

ROUND 1: Ch 3, 3 dc in ring, ch 4, (4 dc in ring, ch 4) three times, join with sl st to top ch 3.

ROUND 2: Sc in turning ch and next 3 dc, (6 sc in ch-4-sp, sc in next 4 dc) three times, join with sl st to first sc. Fasten off.

ROUND 3: Switch to Yarn A. Sl st to join between 2nd and 3rd sc on previous round. Ch 4, dc in same st. Ch 10, (dc between 2nd and 3rd sc of next group, ch 1, dc in same place, ch 10) three times, join with sl st in 3rd st of ch 4.

ROUND 4: Sl st to 1st ch-10-sp, work 15 sc over ch-10-sp, ch 5, (15 sc over next ch-10-sp, ch 5) three times, do not join.

ROUND 5: Skip the first sc, sc in each of next 13 sc, skip final sc in group, ch 5, sc in ch-5-sp, ch 5, (skip 1st sc, sc in next 13 sc, skip final sc, ch 5, 1 sc in ch-5-sp) three times more. Do not join.

ROUND 6: (Skip the first sc, sc in each of next 11 sc, skip final sc in group, ch 5, sc in ch-5-sp, ch 5, sc in ch-5-sp, ch 5) four times around, join with sl st to second sc of round. Fasten off. Weave in ends.

FOREST PATH SKIRT SCHEMATIC

15 "

36 [40, 44, 48] "

INSTRUCTIONS

Obtaining proper gauge for each square, after blocking, is essential for creating a skirt of the exact size desired. Make sure your gauge is correct before continuing!

Work 36 (40, 44, 48) squares. Steam block.

ASSEMBLY

Sew squares into a rectangle 9 (10, 11, 12) squares long and 4 squares high. Sew up remaining short end to make tube. Sew in ends.

WAISTBAND

Worked in rounds without turning.

ROUND 1: Reattach Yarn A with sl st to top center of a square. (Ch 9, sc in next ch-sp, ch 6, dc in next 2 ch-sp, ch 6, sc in next ch-sp, ch 9, sl st to center sc of square) around top edge of skirt. Join with sc into beginning sl st.

ROUND 2: 3 sl st in first ch-sp, (sc in ch-sp, ch 6) around.

ROUND 3: As for round 2.

ROUND 4: Ch 1, 3 sc in each ch-sp around, sl st to join.

ROUNDS 5–10: Ch 2, hdc around, sl st to join.

Fasten off.

FINISHING

Weave in any ends. Steam block lightly. Sew in a lining if desired, or wear over leggings or purchased slip.

CHAPTER FOUR

LITTLE LUXURIES

sensual accessories for dressing up

vintage lace
SCARF

dana codding

SIZES
ONE SIZE

FINISHED MEASUREMENTS
6" by 44"

YARN
Schaefer Andrea (100% cultured silk; 1093yds/100g): 1 skein, variegated blue/purple/green

SUBSTITUTION: Approximately 328 yds lace-weight yarn

HOOKS
US 8/1.5mm steel thread crochet hook or size to achieve gauge

NOTIONS
Very small yarn needle or embroidery needle

GAUGE
When blocked, each motif measures 2¼" square. Gauge is not significant; heavier yarns will give a larger stole.

I've never been happy wearing large triangular shawls. They always seem to slide off my shoulders and get in the way. With that in mind, I set out to make a tiny scarf—just enough to drape over my shoulders and provide a touch of something special to any little black dress. This sliver of silk, crisp and luscious, is just the thing to set off any formal outfit or provide a touch of sensuality to a T-shirt and jeans. You can crochet it in wool if you like, but it won't have the same sheen as pure silk! If you prefer a larger scarf, just work more motifs until you're satisfied.

Dana Codding is a geologist and knitting teacher living in Calgary, Alberta. She enjoys updating old knitting and crochet patterns and playing with texture.

SPECIAL STITCHES

CL (CLUSTER): tr into next 5 tr, holding back last loop of each tr on hook—5 loops on hook; yo and draw yarn through all 5 loops

JOIN: join with a sl st to close round

STITCH PATTERN

SINGLE MOTIF

ROUND 1: Ch 11. Join.

ROUND 2: 16 sc into ring. Join.

ROUND 3: Ch 4, 4 tr into same sc as join. *Ch 2, skip 1 sc, 5 tr into next sc* 7 times. Ch 2, join to top stitch of ch 4—8 groups of tr made.

ROUND 4: Ch 4, tr into next 4 tr, holding back last loop of each tr and last ch of ch 4 on hook. 5 loops on hook. Yo and draw through all 5 loops. Ch 16. *Skip 2 ch-sp, cl, Ch 10, skip 2ch-sp, cl, ch 16* to last set of tr, cl, ch 10, join to top ch of ch 4.

JOINING TO ONE MOTIF

Work rounds 1–3 of single motif.

ROUND 4: Ch 4, tr into next 4 tr, holding back last loop of each tr and last loop of ch4 on hook. 5 loops on hook. Yo and draw through all 5 loops. Ch 8, sl st to join to ch-16-sp on prior motif, ch 8. Skip 2 ch-sp, cl, ch 5, sl stitch to join to ch-10-sp on prior motif, ch 5, skip 2 ch-sp, cl, Ch 8, sl st to join to ch-16-sp on prior motif, ch 8. Joining complete. *Skip 2 ch-sp, cl, ch 10, skip 2 ch-sp, cl, ch 16. Repeat from * to last set of tr, cl, ch 10, join to top ch of ch 4.

JOINING TO TWO MOTIFS

Work rounds 1–3 of single motif.

ROUND 4: Ch 4, tr into next 4 tr, holding back last loop of each tr and last loop of ch 4 on hook. 5 loops on hook. Yo and draw through all 5 loops. *Ch 8, sl st to join to ch-16-sp on prior motif, ch 8. Skip 2 ch-sp, cl, ch 5, sl st to join to ch-10-sp on prior motif, ch 5, skip 2 ch-sp, cl. Repeat from * once more. Ch 8, sl st to join to ch-16-sp on prior motif, ch 8. Joining complete. *Skip 2 ch-sp, cl, ch 10, skip 2 ch-sp, cl, ch 16. Repeat from * to last set of tr, cl, ch 10, join to top ch of ch 4.

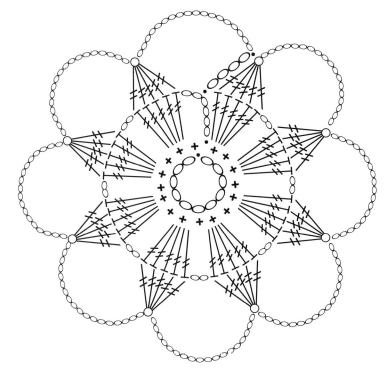

a	3	2	1

b	3	2	1
			4

c	3	2	1
	6	5	4

SCARF

ROW 1: Make first motif as per stitch pattern, above.

Second and third motifs:

Work "Joining to One Motif," above (see Diagram A). Three motifs (one row) made.

ROW 2:

First motif:

Work "Joining to One Motif," above. Join to motif 1 (see Diagram B).

Second and third motifs:
Work "Joining to Two Motifs," above. Join to the corner between 2 and 4, then the corner between 5 and 3 (see Diagram C).

Repeat Row 2 until 22 rows have been completed or stole measures 44" long.

FINISHING

With yarn needle, weave in ends securely.

Soak scarf in warm water and block severely to measurements.

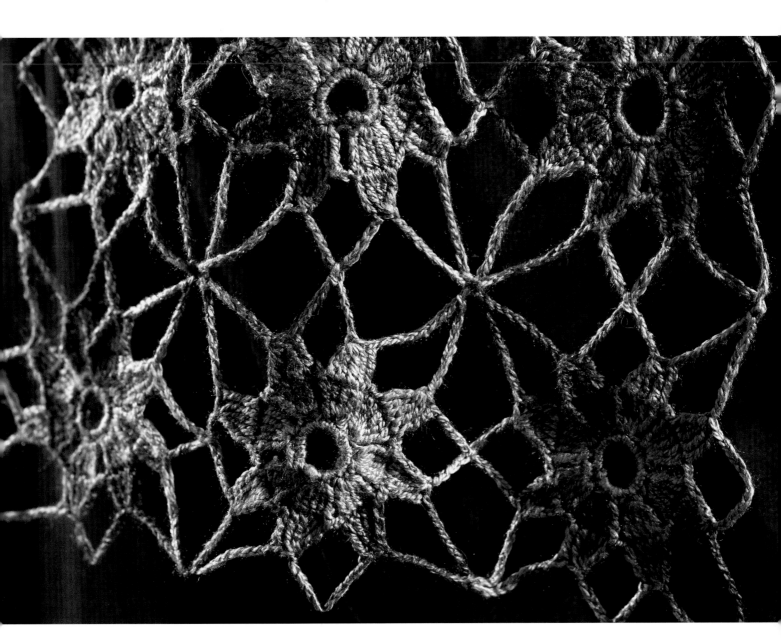

sanctuary
BOLERO

amy swenson

A cropped, contemporary lace bolero-style cardigan works just as well over a sexy cocktail dress as it does with a cami and jeans for daytime wear. Crocheted in a luxe hand-dyed silk/merino blend, it feels amazing close to the skin. The fronts are shaped into a cutaway style, and the sleeves are cropped to the elbows for a practical year-round appeal.

pattern notes

Fit is meant to be slightly smaller than your actual chest measurement.

SIZES

S (M, L, XL)

FINISHED MEASUREMENTS

CHEST: 32 (35, 37½, 40)"

YARN

Alchemy Sanctuary (70% merino wool, 30% silk; 125yds/50g): 7 (8, 8, 9) skeins, Deep Sea (02w)

SUBSTITUTION: Approximately 875–1312 yds sport-weight yarn. Look for yarn that knits to 23–25 sts/4".

HOOKS

US E/3.5mm crochet hook, or size needed to obtain proper gauge

NOTIONS

Yarn needle

GAUGE

To work a proper gauge swatch for this project:

Ch 22 sts.

Work rows 1–3 of stitch pattern, then rows 2 and 3 twice more.

Gently block.

Your swatch should measure 4" wide and 4" tall.

SPECIAL STITCH

V-ST (V-STITCH): (2 dc, ch 1, 2 dc)

CONTEMPORARY LACE PATTERN

Worked over a multiple of 6 sts plus 4.

LACE ROW 1: V-st in 6th ch from hook, (ch 1, skip 6 ch, V-st in next ch) repeat to last 3 ch, end with V-st, skip 2 ch, dc in last ch. Turn.

LACE ROW 2: Ch 3, [V-st in prev. V-st, (ch, sc, ch) in next ch-sp] repeat to last V-st, end with V-st in last V-st, dc in turning ch. Turn.

LACE ROW 3: Ch 3, (V-st in prev. ch-sp, ch 1) to last V-st, end with V-st in last V-st, dc in turning ch. Turn.

Repeat rows 2 and 3 for stitch pattern.

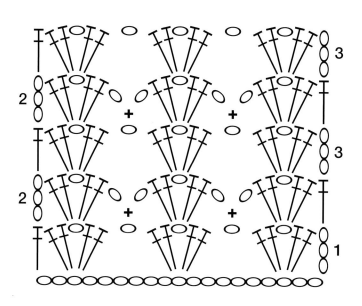

BACK

Ch 76 (82, 88, 94).

Work in Contemporary Lace stitch pattern until piece measures 6", end having just finished row 3.

ARMHOLE SHAPING

SHAPING ROW 1: Ch 1, work sc in ea. st and ch-sp of first V-st, sc in next ch-sp (dec. made), beginning with ch 1, continue in row 2 of pattern for 10 (11, 12, 13) repeats, end with ch 1, sc in ch-sp before last V-st. Turn.

SHAPING ROW 2: Ch 1, sl st in 1st dc, sc in next dc and sc in ch-sp, ch 4, 2 dc in same ch-sp, continue in row 3 of lace pattern. In last V-st, 2 dc ch 1, dc last ch-sp. Turn.

SHAPING ROW 3: Ch 4, 2 dc in 1st ch-sp, work in row 2 of lace pattern to last V-st, end with 2 dc ch 1, dc in last ch-sp**, turn.

Continue even, repeating Shaping Row 3, until armhole measures 6½ (7, 7½, 8)" from start of shaping, ending having just completed row 3 of stitch pattern.

SHAPE BACK NECK

ROW 1: Ch 4, 2 dc in 1st ch-sp, ch 1, sc in next ch-sp, ch 1, V-st in next ch-sp, ch 1, sc in ch-sp, ch 1, 2 dc in ch-sp. Turn.

ROW 2: Ch 1, V-st in 3rd ch-sp, ch 1, V-st in last ch-sp. Fasten off.

Reattach yarn to other arm edge, work last two rows again to complete other side of neck shaping.

FRONT LEFT

Ch 16 (22, 28, 34).

Work Lace Row 1. Turn.

LEFT FRONT INCREASES

INCREASE ROW 1: Work lace row 2 to end of row; V-st in turning ch. Turn.

INCREASE ROW 2: Ch 4, 2 dc in 1st ch-sp, ch 1, continue as for lace row 3 to end. Turn.

INCREASE ROW 3: Work lace row 2 to end of row, V-st turning ch. Turn.

INCREASE ROW 4: Ch 4, work as for lace row 3 to end. Turn.

Repeat Increase Rows 1–4 once more, then Increase Rows 1–3 once more.

On next row, ch 3, work as for Lace Row 3 to end. Turn.

ARMHOLE SHAPING

Work armhole shaping as for back, finishing where marked with **.

Work 2 rows even, in lace pattern.

NECK SHAPING

ROW 1: Ch 1, sl st in 2nd dc, ch 2, 2 dc in ch-sp, continue across row as for lace row 3. Turn.

ROW 2: Ch 4, 2 dc in next ch-sp [(ch 1, sc, in next ch-sp, ch 1), V-st in next ch-sp] 2(3, 4, 5) times, ch 1, sc in ch-sp, ch 1, dc in last ch-sp. Turn.

ROW 3: Ch 1, work as for lace row 3. Turn.

ROW 4: Ch 4, 2 dc in next ch-sp [(ch 1, sc in next ch-sp, ch 1), V-st in next ch-sp] 1(2, 3, 4) times, ch 1, sc in next ch-sp, ch 1, dc in last ch-sp. Turn.

ROW 5: Ch 3, work as for Lace Row 3. Turn.

ch 1), V-st in next ch-sp)] 2 times, ch 1, sc in ch-sp, ch 1, dc in last ch-sp. Turn.

ROW 8: Ch 1, work as for Lace Row 3. Turn.

ROW 9: Ch 4, 2 dc in ch-sp [(ch 1, sc in next ch-sp, ch 1), V-st in next ch-sp)] 1 time, ch 1, sc in ch-sp, ch 1, dc in last ch-sp. Turn.

ROW 10: Ch 3, work as for row 3. Turn.

FOR SIZE XL ONLY

ROW 6: Ch 1, sl st in 2nd dc, ch 2, 2 dc in ch-sp, continue across row as for lace row 3. Turn.

ROW 7: Ch 4, 2 dc in ch-sp [(ch 1, sc in next ch-sp, ch 1), V-st in next ch-sp)] 3 times, ch 1, sc in ch-sp, ch 1, dc in last ch-sp. Turn.

ROW 8: Ch 1, work as for Lace Row 3. Turn.

ROW 9: Ch 4, 2 dc in ch-sp [(ch 1, sc in next ch-sp, ch 1), V-st in next ch-sp)] 2 times, ch 1, sc in ch-sp, ch 1, dc in last ch-sp. Turn.

ROW 10: Ch 3, work as for Lace Row 3. Turn.

ROW 11: Ch 4, 2 dc in ch-sp [(ch 1, sc in next ch-sp, ch 1), V-st in next ch-sp)] 1 time, ch 1, sc in ch-sp, ch 1, dc in last ch-sp. Turn.

ROW 12: Ch 1, work as for Lace Row 3. Turn.

FOR ALL SIZES

Work even, repeating rows 2 and 3 of lace pattern until front matches same length as back to shoulder. Fasten off.

FRONT RIGHT

Ch 15 (21, 27, 33).

Work row 1 of Contemporary Lace stitch pattern. Turn.

FRONT INCREASE ROWS

INCREASE ROW 1: Ch 4, 2 dc in 1st ch-sp, continue as for Lace Row 2 to end. Turn.

INCREASE ROW 2: Work Lace Row 3 to last 4 dc, ch 1, skip 4dc, V-st in final ch-4-sp. Turn.

INCREASE ROW 3: Ch 3, (dc, ch 1, 2 dc) in 1st ch-sp, continue as for row 2 to end. Turn.

INCREASE ROW 4: Work Lace Row 3 to last st, ch 1, dc in last dc. Turn.

Repeat last 4 rows twice more.

ARMHOLE SHAPING

Work armhole shaping as for back, finishing where marked with **, as for row 2 of lace pattern.

Work 2 rows even, as for lace pattern.

FOR SIZE M ONLY

ROW 6: Ch 1, sl st in 2nd dc, ch 2, 2 dc in ch-sp, continue across row as for Lace Row 3. Turn.

ROW 7: Ch 4, 2 dc in ch-sp [(ch 1, sc in next ch-sp, ch 1), V-st in next ch-sp)] 1 time, ch 1, sc in ch-sp, ch 1, dc in last ch-sp. Turn.

ROW 8: Ch 1, work as for Lace Row 3. Turn.

FOR SIZE L ONLY

ROW 6: Ch 1, sl st in 2nd dc, ch 2, 2 dc in ch-sp, continue across row as for Lace Row 3. Turn.

ROW 7: Ch 4, 2 dc in ch-sp [(ch 1, sc in next ch-sp,

NECK SHAPING

SIZE S ONLY

ROW 1: Work as for Lace Row 3 to final V-st, 2 dc in ch-sp, ch 2, sl st in 2nd dc.

ROW 2: Ch 1, sl st in 1st ch-sp and dc, ch 4, sc in ch-sp, ch 1, finish row as for Lace Row 2. Turn.

ROW 3: Work as for Lace Row 3. Turn.

ROW 4: Ch 1, sl st in 1st 2 dc and ch-sp, ch 4, sc in ch-sp, ch 1, finish row as for Lace Row 2. Turn.

ROW 5: Ch 4, 2 dc in ch-sp, ch 1, V-st in next V-st, dc in ch-4-sp. Turn.

SIZE M ONLY

ROW 1: Work as for Lace Row 3 to final V-st, 2 dc in ch-sp, ch 2, sl st in 2nd dc. Turn.

ROW 2: Ch 1, sl st in 1st ch-sp and dc, ch 4, sc in ch-sp, ch 1, finish row as for Lace Row 2. Turn.

ROW 3: Work as for Lace Row 3. Turn.

ROW 4: Ch 1, sl st in 1st 2 dc and ch-sp, ch 4, sc in ch-sp, ch 1, finish row as for Lace Row 2. Turn.

ROW 5: Ch 4, 2 dc in ch-sp, ch 1, V-st in next two V-sts, dc in ch-4-sp. Turn.

ROW 6: Ch 1, sl st in 1st ch-sp and dc, ch 4, sc in ch-sp, ch 1, finish row as for Lace Row 2. Turn.

ROW 7: Work as for Lace Row 3. Turn.

SIZE L ONLY

ROW 1: Work as for Lace Row 3 to final V-st, 2 dc in last ch-sp, ch 2, sl st in 2nd dc. Turn.

ROW 2: Ch 1, sl st in 1st ch-sp and 1st dc, ch 4, sc in next ch-sp, ch 1, finish as for Lace Row 2. Turn.

ROW 3: Work as for Lace Row 3. Turn.

ROW 4: Ch 1, sl st in 1st 2 dc and ch-sp, ch 4, sc in ch-sp, ch 1, finish as for Lace Row 2. Turn.

ROW 5: Ch 4, 2 dc in ch-sp, ch 1, V-st in ea. of next two V-sts, dc in ch-4-sp. Turn.

ROW 6: Ch 1, sl st in 1st ch-sp and dc, ch 4, sc in ch-sp, ch 1, finish as for Lace Row 2. Turn.

ROW 7: Work as for Lace Row 3. Turn.

ROW 8: Ch 1, sl st in 1st 2 dc and ch-sp, ch 4, sc in ch-sp, ch 1, finish as for Lace Row 2. Turn.

ROW 9: Ch 4, 2 dc in ch-sp, ch 1, V-st in next V-st, dc in ch-4-sp. Turn.

ROW 10: Ch 1, sl st in 1st ch-sp and dc, ch 4, sc in next ch-sp, ch 1, finish as for Lace Row 2. Turn.

ROW 11: Work as for Lace Row 3. Turn.

SIZE XL ONLY

ROW 1: Work as for Lace Row 3 to final V-st, 2 dc in ch-sp, ch 2, sl st in 2nd dc. Turn.

ROW 2: Ch 1, sl st in 1st ch-sp and dc, ch 4, sc in ch-sp, ch 1, finish as for Lace Row 2. Turn.

ROW 3: Work as for Lace Row 3. Turn.

ROW 4: Ch 1, sl st in 1st 2 dc and ch-sp, ch 4, sc in ch-sp, ch 1, finish as for Lace Row 2. Turn.

ROW 5: Ch 4, 2 dc in ch-sp, ch 1, V-st in each of next 3 V-sts, dc in ch-4-sp. Turn.

ROW 6: Ch 1, sl st in 1st ch-sp and dc, ch 4, sc in ch-sp, ch 1, finish as for Lace Row 2. Turn.

ROW 7: Work as for Lace Row 3. Turn.

ROW 8: Ch 1, sl st in 1st 2 dc and ch-sp, ch 4, sc in ch-sp, ch 1, finish as for Lace Row 2. Turn.

ROW 9: Ch 4, 2 dc in ch-sp, ch 1, V-st in next 2 V-sts, dc in ch-4-sp. Turn.

ROW 10: Ch 1, sl st in 1st 2 dc and ch-sp, ch 4, sc in ch-sp, ch 1, finish row as for Lace Row 2. Turn.

ROW 11: Ch 4, 2 dc in ch-sp, ch 1, V-st in next V-st, dc in ch-4-sp. Turn.

ROW 12: Ch 1, sl st in 1st ch-sp and dc, ch 4, sc in ch-sp, ch 1, finish row as for Lace Row 2. Turn.

ROW 13: Work as for Lace Row 3. Turn.

FOR ALL SIZES

Continue even in lace pattern as set, until front matches same length as back to the shoulders. Fasten off.

SLEEVES

Make 2.

Ch 58 (58, 64, 64).

Beginning with Lace Row 1, work in stitch pattern until sleeve measures 4½" from beginning, end having just completed Lace Row 2.

SLEEVE SHAPING

INCREASE ROW 1: Ch 3, dc in top of first dc, ch 1, work as for Lace Row 3, end with ch 1, 2 dc in turning ch. Turn.

INCREASE ROW 2: Ch 3, dc in 1st dc, ch 1, sc in ch-sp, ch 1, work as for Lace Row 2 to last ch-1-sp, ch 1, sc in ch-sp, ch 1, 2 dc in turning ch. Turn.

INCREASE ROW 3: Ch 3, dc in top of first dc, ch 1, work as for Lace Row 3 to last ch-3-sp, ch 1, 2 dc in turning ch. Turn.

INCREASE ROW 4: Ch 3, dc in 1st dc, ch 1, sc in ch-sp, ch 1, work as for Lace Row 2 to last ch-1-sp, ch 1, sc in ch-sp, ch 1, 2 dc in turning ch. Turn.

INCREASE ROW 5: Ch 4, 2 dc in top of 1st dc, ch 1, work as for Lace Row 3 end with V-st in turning ch. Turn.

INCREASE ROW 6: Ch 3, V-st in first ch-sp, work as for Lace Row 2 to end, V-st in turning ch. Turn.

INCREASE ROW 7: Work as for Lace Row, placing final dc in turning ch. Turn.

INCREASE ROW 8: As for row 2 of stitch pattern. Turn.

Work rows 1–8 of increase pattern 2 (2, 3, 3) times, then work Lace Row 3 once.

SHAPE SLEEVE CAP

ROW 1: Ch 4, sc in 1st ch-sp, ch 1, in next in V-st, (ch 1, sc, ch 1) in next ch-sp, work as for Lace Row 2 to last half V-st, dc in turning ch. Turn.

ROW 2: Ch 3, work as for Lace Row 3, placing final dc in turning ch-4. Turn.

ROW 3: Ch 2, sc in 2nd and 3rd dc, ch 2, 2dc in ch-sp, work as for Lace Row 2 to last V-st, 2 dc in ch-sp. Turn.

Repeat last 2 rows 3 (3, 3, 4) times more. Fasten off.

FINISHING

Steam block lightly. Sew shoulder seams. Sew sleeve caps into armholes. Sew up sleeves and side seams. Weave in ends.

NECK EDGING

Beginning at back right edge of neck, attach yarn with a sl st. Working evenly around entire front edge of bolero, work one row of sc. Sl st to join.

Fasten off.

SANCTUARY BOLERO SCHEMATIC

9"

32 [35, 37.5, 40] "

outside the lines
SCARF

amy o'neill houck

Alpaca and silk blended together make for sensual crocheting indeed. Your hook glides effortlessly, and drape is achieved without worry. This little piece was inspired by my love of lines and boxes (when my mind wanders that's what you'll find me doodling). Wear this little beauty as a scarf, or wind it around your waist for a trend-setting style.

SIZES

ONE SIZE

FINISHED MEASUREMENTS

LENGTH: 36", including ruffled edge

WIDTH: 4" after blocking

RUFFLE WIDTH: 8" at widest point after blocking

YARN

Blue Sky Alpacas Alpaca/Silk (50% alpaca, 50% silk; 146yds/50g): 1 hank, White (120)

SUBSTITUTION: Approximately 142 yds sport-weight yarn that knits to 24 sts/4" in Stockinette stitch.

HOOKS

US G/4.0 mm crochet hook

NOTIONS

Yarn needle

GAUGE

16 sc to 4" on 4mm hook

pattern notes

Gauge is not essential with this scarf since there is no sizing, but if your gauge is significantly larger than what's listed, you will need more yarn.

This pattern is designed to create a short piece that you wear right at the neck or stretch to tie around your waist. If you have more yarn and want a longer scarf, you can make your foundation row as long as you'd like your piece to be (minus the ruffle), just make sure your foundation is a multiple of 4, plus 2.

This project uses Foundation Single Crochet (fsc) which creates a first row of sc without a chain. That way, you don't have one part of your project that has less stretch and give (foundation chains can often be too tight). This technique is ideal for this scarf that's worked out from the center because you can easily work another row off the backside of the foundation. Once you've mastered the technique you'll find yourself applying it to lots of different projects. See the Special Stitches section below to learn how to create it.

Amy O'Neill Houck is a writer and designer of crochet and knitwear. She learned to crochet from her grandmother when she was eight years old and favored making silly hats up until she began designing professionally in 2002. Amy's writing and designs have been featured in Crochet Today, Interweave Crochet, *and* Crochet Me, *as well as with yarn companies and in many books. She is the author of the forthcoming* Color Book of Felted Crochet, *and she blogs at* The Hook and I *(hookandi.blogspot.com).*

SPECIAL STITCHES

SHELL: 8 dc all worked in the ch-sp indicated

FSC (FOUNDATION SINGLE CROCHET): ch 2, insert hook into 2nd ch from hook, draw up a loop, ch 1, yo, pull through both loops on hook; *insert hook into ch-1 just made, draw up a loop, ch 1, yo, pull through both loops on hook, repeat from * to form fsc

SCARF

NOTE: Turning chain counts as dc. St directly below is skipped throughout the pattern. When the ch is longer than 3 sts, the first 3 sts are the turning ch.

Work 91 fsc. Turn.

ROW 1: Ch 5. Dc in 4th st, *ch 2, skip 2 sts, dc in next st. Repeat from * to the end of the row, turn.

ROW 2: Ch 3, shell (8 dc) in 2nd ch-sp, *skip 2 ch-sp, shell, repeat from * until only 1 ch-sp remains. Dc in turning ch. Turn.

ROWS 3–4: Repeat rows 1–2. Fasten off.

Flip scarf over. Join yarn to backside of fsc and repeat rows 1–4. Do not fasten off.

RUFFLE

ROW 1: Ch 3. Turn scarf so you're working down the ends of the rows. Work 42 dc along the end of the scarf. Turn.

ROW 2: Ch 4, dc in 3rd st, *ch 1, skip 1 st, dc in next st. Repeat from * to the end of the row. Turn.

ROW 3: Ch 4, *dc in next ch-sp, ch 1, repeat from * to end of row, end with dc in turning ch.

ROWS 4–9: Repeat row 3.

Fasten off. Join yarn at other end of scarf and repeat ruffle.

FINISHING

Weave in ends.

chunky alpaca
SHRUG

amy swenson

SIZES

S–M (L–XL)

FINISHED MEASUREMENTS

48 (52)" from cuff to cuff

YARN

Misti Alpaca Chunky (100% baby alpaca; 108yds/100g): 3 (4) skeins, Natural Cream (100)

SUBSTITUTION: Approximately 273 (383) yds chunky-weight yarn. Look for yarn that knits to 12–14 sts/4".

HOOKS

US J/6.0mm crochet hook, or size needed to obtain proper gauge

NOTIONS

Yarn needle

GAUGE

12 sc to 4"

Crocheted in ultrasoft baby alpaca, this openwork shrug drapes gracefully and softly while providing just enough warmth for a special night out or a cozy evening inside by the fire. This shrug uses a supersimple stitch pattern and virtually no shaping, making this pattern ideal for new crocheters or those wanting an instant-gratification project. Choose any chunky yarn. I especially like the chunky alpaca for its fuzzy and glamorous warmth.

pattern notes

The sizing on this shrug can be controlled during seaming. Because you are simply crocheting a large rectangle, it can be sewn to accommodate for your specific size. Be sure to try it on over what you plan on wearing as part of the ensemble!

Pattern is worked in one piece from cuff to cuff and sewn together to make the shrug. Shrug is then finished with rounds of sc around front edge after seaming.

TRIANGLE MESH STITCH

Worked over a multiple of 6 sts.

ROW 1: Ch 7, sc in 3rd sc, *skip 2 sc (ch 3, tr, ch 3) in next sc, skip 2 sc, sc in next sc, repeat from * to last 3 sc, ch 3, tr in final sc. Turn.

ROW 2: Ch 3, (tr in next sc, ch 2, sc in tr, ch 3) to final ch7-sp, sc in ch-sp. Turn.

ROW 3: Ch 7, (sc in tr, ch 3, tr in sc, ch 3) to last tr, sc in tr, ch 3, tr in ch3-sp. Turn.

SHRUG

Ch 43 (49).

ROW 1: Sc in 2nd and every following ch; 42 (48) sc.

ROW 2: Ch 1, sc in each sc across.

Repeat row 2 3 more times for a total of 5 rows.

Begin Triangle Mesh pattern, work rows 1 through 3, then repeat rows 2 and 3 until shrug measures 48 (52)" from fsc, ending after a row 2.

FINAL CUFF

ROW 1: Ch 1, sc in 1st sc, (2 sc in ch-2-sp, sc in tr, 2 sc in ch-2-sp, sc in sc) to last sc, 2 sc in ch-2-sp, sc in tr, 2 sc in ch-3-sp; 42 (48) sc.

ROW 2: Ch 1, sc in each sc across.

Repeat row 2 3 more times for a total of 5 rows.

Fasten off.

FINISHING

Fold shrug rectangle in half so side edges are touching. Beginning at one cuff, sew seam for arm for 17". Repeat from second cuff to create other sleeve. At this point it's a good idea to try the shrug on to make sure enough room is left for your shoulders. If the shrug seems too baggy, continue to sew up the sleeves a little longer.

Beginning at one seam, reattach yarn with a sl st, ch 1, and sc evenly around front opening. Work 3 more rounds of sc. Fasten off. Weave in ends.

petite bijoux
BAG

amy swenson

SIZES

ONE SIZE

FINISHED MEASUREMENTS

Approximately 10" in diameter and 6" deep, with a drawstring closure

YARN

Tilli Tomas Simply Heaven (100% silk; 120yds/100g): 1 skein, American Beauty

SUBSTITUTION: Approximately 109 yds chunky-weight silk. Look for yarn that knits to 12–16 sts/4".

HOOKS

US G7/4.5mm crochet hook

NOTIONS

Yarn needle

GAUGE

Exact gauge is not important for this project; just make sure to be working a sufficiently dense fabric.

With one perfect skein of chunky pure silk and a few hours of spare time, you can whip up this little drawstring evening bag. The perfect size for your lipstick, driver's license, and credit card, the Petite Bijoux Bag is designed to dangle seductively from your wrist all night long. Need a larger bag? Grab another skein and continue making the base of the bag wider before continuing up the sides.

BASE OF BAG

Ch 2, work 8 sc in 2nd ch from hook. Do not sl st. You'll be working the base of the bag in spiral rounds.

Increases: (Sc in first sc, 2 sc in next sc) 45 times.

Work Even: Sc in each sc 54 times.

SIDES OF BAG

(Ch 1, sc in next sc) 27 times, then continue around, working ch 1, sc in each ch-sp until bag is 6" from base, or to desired height.

EYELET ROUND FOR DRAWSTRING

Ch 2, (dc in next ch-sp, ch 1) to begining of round, sl st in ch-2.

RUFFLE

Ch 3, 2 dc in ch-sp, 3 dc in every ch-sp to end of round, sl st in ch-3 to join.

Ch 3, dc in every dc around.

Fasten off.

FINISHING

TIES

Make 2.

With double strand of silk, ch 60, leaving a 6" tail on either end. Weave chain through eyelets, and tie loose ends together on the inside of the bag. Use needle to sew ends to inside of bag, attaching strap.

Weave in ends.

APPENDIX

abbreviations, references, and yarn sources

ABBREVIATIONS

( )	alternate measurements and/or instructions
* *	repeat all instructions between asterisks
blo	back loop only
ch	chain
ch-sp	the space made by one or more chain stitches
dc	double triple
dec(s)('d)	decrease(s); decreasing; decreased
dtr	double treble
g	gram(s)
hdc	half double crochet
inc(s)('d)	increase(s); increasing; increased
m	marker
RS	right side
sc	single crochet
sl st	slip(ped) stitch
sp(s)	space(es)
st(s)	(stitch(es)
tog	together
tr	triple crochet
WS	wrong side
yd(s)	yard(s)
yo	yarn over hook

SYMBOLCRAFT SYMBOL DEFINITIONS

- • Slip stitch
- ✚ Single Crochet
- ○ Chain
- ✝ Half Double Crochet
- ┬ Double Crochet
- ⟋ Triple Crochet
- ≡ Double Triple Crochet

MEASUREMENT CONVERSIONS

unit	multiply by	to get
cm	.394	inch
inch	2.54	cm
meter	1.09	yards
yard	.9144	meters
ounce	28.35	grams
gram	.353	ounces

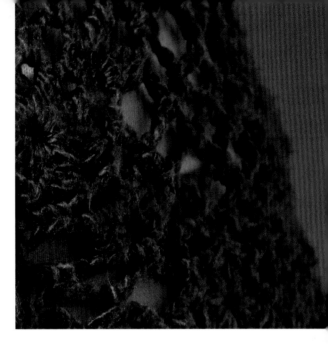

REFERENCES

Whether you're already an A+ crocheter or just getting "hooked," it's always a good idea to keep a few references on hand.

GENERAL INSTRUCTION AND STITCH GUIDES

These books are a great place to start if you need to learn the basic stitches and finishing techniques, or want to find out more about different stitch combinations.

Not Your Mama's Crochet

(Wiley, 2006)

Amy Swenson
Written by *Sensual Crochet* author Amy Swenson, this book assumes you know nothing, but gives you all the nitty-gritty detail on crochet.

Teach Yourself Visually: Crochet

(Wiley, 2006)

Kim Werker and Cecily Keim
This full-color how-to book has photos for every step of the game. Great for visual learners!

Donna Kooler's Encyclopedia of Crochet

(Leisure Arts, 2002)

Donna Kooler
The first 50 pages of this massive volume cover crochet basics, and the last 100 pages, stitch patterns from ripples to grannies. Everything in between are variations on simple patterns. Donna's stitch patterns are accompanied by large color photographs, and include written instructions as well as full-color Symbolcraft Charts

The Crochet Stitch Bible

(Krause, 2004)

Betty Barnden
Over 200 traditional and contemporary stitch patterns are presented in this small coil-bound book. Betty also gives you just enough information to get started if you've never before picked up a hook. A great reference, and small enough to fit in your crochet bag.

The Crocheter's Companion

(Interweave Press, 2006)

Nancy Brown
The updated edition of this crocheter's classic is hardbound for a longer life. The 100-some pages of information are formatted into a flip-style design, meant to stand open on your desk or table as you work. Common questions, from working in rounds to Tunisian crochet, are covered in this handy little volume.

REFERENCES ONLINE

Hooked up to the Web? Check out these sites for more crochet help and inspiration.

Crochetme Magazine

www.crochetme.com
This hip and happening online crochet 'zine publishes patterns and articles quarterly.

Crochet Pattern Central

www.crochetpatterncentral.com
Perhaps the Internet's largest collection of stitch patterns, Crochet Pattern Central has stitch guides, vintage patterns, forums, and more.

Interweave Crochet

www.interweavecrochet.com
One of the most popular knitting periodicals has recently launched a crochet-only magazine, found on newsstands 4 times a year. Their companion site features articles, free patterns, and more. Expect high-end yarns and fashionable designs.

YARN SOURCES

None of the designs in this book would have been possible without the luxurious yarns provided by the following companies. To find these yarns, look in your local yarn shop, or contact the companies below to obtain a list of retail stores stocking their yarns.

Alchemy Yarns of Transformation
www.alchemyyarns.com

Artyarns
www.artyarns.com

Blue Sky Alpacas
www.blueskyalpacas.com

Cascade Yarns
www.cascadeyarns.com

Curious Creek Fibers
www.curiouscreek.com

Handmaiden
www.handmaiden.ca

Jade Sapphire
www.jadesapphire.com

Karabella
www.karabellayarns.com

Lorna's Laces
www.lornaslaces.net

Misti Alpaca International
www.mistialpaca.com

Rowan
www.knitrowan.com

Rowan Yarn Classics
www.ryclassics.com

Schaefer Yarns
www.schaeferyarn.com

South West Trading Company
www.soysilk.com

Tilli Tomas
www.tillitomas.com

ACKNOWLEDGMENTS

Ahead of anyone, Alana Marchetto deserves special thanks for furiously crocheting a significant proportion of the projects photographed in this book. Had she not been crazy enough to agree to help, this book would not have come together on schedule. (Incidentally, she's also a wonderful person and an amazing crochet teacher.) This book's designers—Amie, Amy, Annie, Dana, Debora, and Robyn— provided not only spectacular designs but much-needed inspiration, dedication, and motivation. Amy O'Neill Houck was a stunning technical editor, who managed to whip these 25 patterns into fine form. The folks at Hollan should be thanked not only for the idea to create a glamorous and fashionable crochet book, but also for making all the pieces fall into place. Lastly, to my friends and family, and all those blog readers out there, thank you for lending your feedback and support time and time again. I hope I don't have to say that I'm incredibly proud of the designs in this book. I wish you many happy hours of luxurious crochet.